# PRAISE F

"In an era when business advice is often loud and insistent, this book is a refreshing change. Its quiet wisdom will help you see your professional challenges and opportunities more clearly and find a pathway to greater success and meaning."

> – Daniel H. Pink, #1 New York Times best-selling author of
> *To Sell is Human, Drive,* and *The Power of Regret*

"Exceptionally relevant and as precisely focused on a leader's greatest challenge as its ambitious title. Jim Vaselopulos's *Clarity* is a common-sense primer on the things business leaders face daily. Every story resonated brilliantly."

> – Stan McChrystal, Founder & CEO,
> McChrystal Group General, US Army (Ret)

"What sets visionary leaders apart from the rest of us? *Clarity.* Jim Vaselopulos brings you on a captivating journey to unlock your power and influence so that people will be eager to join in bringing your great ideas to life."

> – Zoe Chance, author of *Influence Is Your Superpower*

"Clarity is the foundation that supports excellence at all levels of an organization. Jim Vaselopulos' book *Clarity* includes wonderful depictions of how to serve your customers, engage your employees, and build true leadership within your organization."

> – Horst Schulze, co-founder of The Ritz-Carlton Hotel Company

"Anyone who actually wants to become an effective leader in business should read this insightful book. Jim Vaselopulos weaves together a set of engaging stories that shed light on organizational complexities and leadership challenges while leading you in recognizing your own challenges and gaining the clarity to resolve them. You will see some part of yourself in every chapter, every section, perhaps even every page -- and find wisdom that leads you to success."

— B. Joseph Pine II, coauthor of, *The Experience Economy: Competing for Customer Time, Attention, and Money*

"Jim's book *Clarity* is delightfully refreshing in the way it walks you through the journeys of three fictional characters, each with a different business dilemma. This unique format is very powerful and displays how interpersonal relationships and influence are critical skill sets for business success. The format is also very impactful in that it takes complex concepts such as wisdom and clarity and makes them approachable and attainable."

— Robert Cialdini, New York Times best-selling author of *Influence* and *Pre-Suasion*

"The foundation for success, especially in demanding conditions, depends upon an ability to discard what is unimportant and focus on what is truly important. I learned these lessons as a fighter pilot, both in training and in combat. Jim's book *Clarity* contains the foundation and the methodology for business leaders to strip away distractions and focus on issues that will move their businesses forward."

— Kim "KC" Campbell, Colonel, U.S. Air Force (Retired) and author of *Flying in the Face of Fear: A Fighter Pilot's Lessons on Leading with Courage*

"When I started Jim's book, I was struck by the bold promise made in the introduction - you'll "grow wiser, work less and win big in business." It didn't take long to realize Jim delivers masterfully! *CLARITY* is loaded with actionable directives. Big thumbs up!"

– Don Yaeger, 11-time New York Times best-selling author

"I found this book to be a refreshing approach to business books and an easy read. The stories are realistic, engaging, and instructive. As the Queen of Clarity, I was delighted to see the importance of questions in each of the stories. Jim's book clearly demonstrates the many disciplines leaders can use to unleash the power of their teams to achieve better and faster results."

– Ann Latham, author of *The Power of Clarity*,
*The Disconnect Principle*, and *The Clarity Papers*

"This is not an ordinary business book. It is not a summary of client interviews, personal successes, or standard consultant advice. Rather, it is a highly readable set of stories and case studies told by fictional characters. The case studies all come together in a seminal final section that brims with insight and inspiration. You will want to spend an evening by the fireplace with this book."

– Kim Cameron, William Russell Kelly
Professor Emeritus of Management & Organizations
Ross School of Business and Professor Emeritus of Higher
Education School of Education University of Michigan

"I'm confident Jim Vaselopulos's *Clarity* will become a go-to guide for professionals. Filled with business lessons from his decades of experience, he makes it digestible and entertaining for the reader by illustrating everyday problems—and effective solutions—into well-crafted, inspiring stories. A must-read for anyone looking to advance their career."

— Andrew LaCivita, award-winning author of
*Interview Intervention* and *The Hiring Prophecies*

"In his new book, Jim shares his hard-earned wisdom in a compelling and enjoyable manner, offering clarity to both current and future leaders, particularly when faced with complex dilemmas. This book will undoubtedly help you maximize your efforts to achieve greater success!"

— Jan Rutherford, Founder, Self-Reliant Leadership®

"In SEAL training we teach our BUD/S candidates to take on the hardest tasks and the biggest goals. We do this by taking seemingly impossible tasks and breaking them down into manageable elements that are easier to understand and master. That is exactly what Jim does with his book *Clarity*. With effective storytelling, compelling case studies, and an organized process, Jim explains how anyone hoping to better understand their business can perform under pressure and chart a clear path forward for them and their business."

— Stephen Drum, author of Life on the X, founder of Breaching Leadership, Master Chief, US Navy SEAL (Ret)

"You can't achieve clarity without curiosity, and the way George's story unfolds throughout the pages of this book piques that needed curiosity. But it doesn't just leave you hanging there, it will lead you through a disciplined process by which assumptions were pressure tested and facts were balanced with emotions. This book is both entertaining and educational—a unique take on the modern business book."

– Harris III, Bestselling Author, Storyteller, and Entrepreneur

"Jim is a deep, strategic thinker, and this book illuminates his thought process to help businesspeople refine and improve their problem-solving skills and outcomes, as well as their approach to living a more fulfilling life."

– Doug Marconnet - Managing Director, Bridgewood Advisors Inc.
(Specialists in Mergers & Acquisitions)

"I've been a fan of Jim Vaselopulos for years! He has done a remarkable job of capturing the emotions that entrepreneurs, CEOs, and business leaders experience through powerful storytelling. The situations were tangible and relevant to anyone who is in a leadership position, or aspires to be. The mixture of insightful business content makes this book necessary reading for any business leader seeking wisdom and clarity."

– Paul Darley, Chairman, CEO & President, W.S. Darley & Co.,
author of *Sold! The Art of Relationship Sales*

"In his book *Clarity*, Jim Vaselopulos shows how to truly achieve more with less. The pages overflow with practical insights and methods for reducing noise and confusion and optimizing output. Jim is an expert at asking insightful and incisive questions, and *Clarity* is a masterclass in learning from him how to create clarity in your life."

– Patrick Emmons - Founder & CEO of DragonSpears

# CLARITY

*Business Wisdom to Work Less and Achieve More*

JIM VASELOPULOS

Publishing support provided by
Ignite Press
5070 N. Sixth St. #189
Fresno, CA 93710
www.IgnitePress.us

ISBN: 979-8-9889564-0-2
ISBN: 979-8-9889564-1-9 (Hardcover)
ISBN: 979-8-9889564-2-6 (E-book)

For bulk purchases and for booking, contact:

Jim Vaselopulos
claritybook@rafti.com
www.businesswisdom.com/clarity

Library of Congress Control Number: 2023913944

Cover design by Jim Vaselopulos
Edited by Zoe Herold
Interior illustrations by Bayley Killmeier
Interior design by Jetlaunch

FIRST EDITION

*This book is dedicated to my parents, Spyros & Katherine.*
*They set the foundation and instilled the values*
*for me to see the world clearly.*

# TABLE OF CONTENTS

# INTRODUCTION

As a business advisor and executive coach, people seek my counsel for something often described as wisdom. What is interesting, however, is that wisdom is not what people ultimately desire. After I've had the opportunity to work with clients, they rarely comment on the wisdom they now possess. What I *do* hear about is the clear way they now view their circumstances– **clarity** is what people truly value.

Clarity can mean different things to different people. For some, it arrives in the form of an answer or a direction. For others, it's understanding the context of a complex situation. For most, however, clarity evokes a calm and focused state of mind with lower stress and diminished anxiety over what to do next.

As satisfying as it is to help people find clarity with their business problems, it's far more rewarding to teach someone how to find their own clarity. And that's the purpose of this book– to describe how I help people find clarity with their unique business problems. So that you, too, can find it for yourself.

As we embark on our journey to find clarity in business contexts, let's start with the end in mind.

This book explores the path toward clarity in five distinct parts:

- <u>Part I</u> – We identify and describe the **symptoms** to look for when diagnosing a situation. This helps us know **WHERE** to look.
- <u>Part II</u> – We identify the **obstacles** –or core business problems– that hold back progress. This helps surface **WHAT** to look for.
- <u>Part III</u> – We identify the powerful **disciplines** that impact our ability to see problems clearly. This helps us know **HOW** to look at the world.
- <u>Part IV</u> – We identify the elements of **awareness** that help us address issues efficiently and effectively. This helps us know **WHEN** to address our problems.
- <u>Part V</u> – We identify the final two elements that help us find **clarity** in our business endeavors. This helps us understand **WHY** things are the way they are.

In an effort to simplify the process of learning about clarity, we will employ one of the most powerful ways to learn– a story. As such, each section of the book follows the journey of a single character that helps us isolate specific learnings within an engaging business case study.

In these case studies, you will meet characters such as Diana, Sam, and George. Diana, an entrepreneur, runs an environmental consulting firm that she founded. Sam is the new vice president of sales for a software company about to go public. And George is the general manager for a manufacturing division that is the backbone of his community. All three face challenges unique to them– and likely familiar to you.

You'll feel their pain. You'll experience their struggles. You'll see them reason through their process of discovery.

You'll see how you can tap into your library of experiences to illuminate a clear path forward toward the success you seek. By the end of this book you'll find increased clarity in complicated situations, a superior focus on what really matters, and greater certainty with your next move. Ultimately, increased clarity will allow you to grow wiser, work less and win big in business.

# PART I

## DIAGNOSING BUSINESS SYMPTOMS

My father had a history of stomach ulcers. I don't quite know the cause, but everyone in the family was aware of the exceptional volume of antacid he consumed. I always assumed it was because of the hard life he chose as an entrepreneur and retail business owner. Arriving in America as an immigrant with fifty dollars in his pocket, he did well to provide for his family, building a successful business and establishing a reputation as a wise counselor to many in the Greek-American community.

On one of his many visits to the doctor, my father complained of stomach pains that were typical of anyone suffering from a history of ulcers. As usual, he expected a prescription renewal, a firm handshake, and a trip to the drug store. On this day, though, that is not what happened.

Dr. Susan Nelson asked her typical questions and got her usual answers. She continued with her normal medical examination which included the uncomfortable pressure she would exert with her fingers pushed deep into his abdomen. She sat my father up on the examining table and let him know his ulcers were not flaring up again. But before any feelings of relief could set in, she told my father that he had what is called a "triple-A": an abdominal aortic aneurysm. Without going into detail, Dr. Nelson let him know it was quite serious and that he was going straight to the hospital and would likely be in surgery within a few hours.

My father and my mother were both taken aback. Why so quick? What could be so urgent? The doctor replied calmly: "Mr. Vaselopulos, you could be on the front steps of the hospital and if your aneurysm bursts, they will not be able to get you into the operating room fast enough to save your life." This conversation set a series of events into motion that consumed our family for months and saved my father's life.

And while we are grateful to the surgeons and nurses that repaired my father's aorta, I am always amazed by the actions of Dr. Nelson on that day. How easy would it have been to go through the motions and refill a prescription for the twentieth time? How skilled do you have to be to know which data to seek and what questions to ask? How disciplined do you have to be to interpret the data before you indulge a hunch? What was so special about Dr. Susan Nelson that allowed her to avoid the very human pitfalls of habit, routine, and conjecture?

It turns out that Dr. Nelson was a teaching doctor. Her skill was not just helping patients, but helping young doctors learn her craft. She had spent the time and had earned a reputation for being able to articulate the nuances in a way that differentiates the average from the great. She took tremendous care to pay attention to the details of the process to seek a proper diagnosis. Ultimately, Dr. Nelson wasn't just a teacher– she was a lifelong student of the process of seeking truth.

This section is dedicated to the process of evaluating symptoms and seeking truth. Much like Dr. Nelson retained her discipline and avoided the dangers of assumption and conjecture, so must the skilled business practitioner. The first step on the path toward clarity is to assess the world around us with clear eyes and the patience to prioritize hard-fought truth over the convenience of easy answers and simple narratives.

Perhaps the best way for us to explore the process by which you may seek clarity is through another story.

# 1

## CASE STUDY – DIANA

Diana is the founder and CEO of an environmental consulting firm she started ten years ago. She is frustrated with problems that seem to be piling up and stress that is frequently overwhelming. Like many executives, Diana is too busy and never seems to have enough hours in the day. There are more than a few evenings when Diana finally sits down and contemplates why she ever started her own business.

Even after the tough days, Diana still loves the mission of her organization, the clients they serve and especially the employees of the firm. The mission of the business has always been a unifying element for the team and the backbone of a culture that has supported their success.

Like most busy executives, Diana has delegated large elements of responsibility to her management team. By delegating some of the more mundane aspects of running a business (scheduling, billing, accounting, etc.), Diana can focus her energy on the big picture items that help her grow and scale her environmental consulting firm.

Part of her current stress and anxiety is from missed expectations and key team members' struggles with accountability. Items she has delegated are lingering unfinished while other priorities and emergencies seem to be occupying key members of her team. Diana increasingly finds herself redirecting her team and taking care of some issues on her own. All this extra activity is exhausting Diana and is even causing her to doubt the capability and commitment of her team.

Her biggest concern, however, is turnover. It's a crisis. Key consultants have been leaving for competitors, disrupting clients, and increasing the workload on those who remain. What's most frustrating is that a new incentive program is proving ineffective, as several employees are negotiating for more compensation. Diana's management team seems paralyzed with their response, leaving Diana unsure if market conditions or problems with her management team are causing this crisis.

Regardless, the loss in productivity and sudden decrease in billable hours are creating cash flow issues while wage increases to retain existing staff are impacting profitability. All Diana can think about is that old saying: When it rains, it pours.

Diana knows that she must involve herself to bring stability to the situation. The business has run smoothly before and Diana knows she can get her business back on track if she can just identify the core problem.

In the meantime, Diana is forced to treat the symptoms until she can buy the time to gather the information that will help her identify what the core issue is.

---

*Does any of this sound familiar? Turnover, missed expectations, and endless streams of new problems?*

*Can you identify a time when you were anxious, frustrated, or stressed like Diana?*

# 2

# THE SYMPTOMS

Diana's story is a combination of many stories I've heard through the years advising companies of all shapes and sizes. As a business owner, parts of this story bring back memories of many important lessons learned from the school of hard knocks.

What is unique about this story is that it encompasses all ten of the most common business symptoms I've observed through the years. This is not to say that these are the *only* symptoms businesses may exhibit– these are just ten of the most common symptoms:

| | |
|---|---|
| Accountability | Conflict |
| Agency | Culture |
| Expectations | Turnover/Retention |
| Alignment | Profitability |
| Being Too Busy | Growth |

Think about all the illnesses a doctor might encounter with their patients. Many might have the same symptoms: fever, chills, headache, fatigue, nausea, and inflammation. The same holds true for the typical problems any business may face.

Business symptoms, however, are very different from medical symptoms in several ways. Perhaps the foremost difference is that medical symptoms are only present at an individual level. A person has a fever, chills, or nausea. And while we may have an outbreak where many people exhibit similar symptoms due to some shared root cause, specific symptoms are not shared by or across multiple individuals.

As such, business symptoms are more complex than medical symptoms because they also appear at an interpersonal as well as an organizational level. Business problems that show symptoms at the organizational level are often characterized by the efficiency of systems, alignment of incentives or declining profitability to name a few. At a team or interpersonal level, business problems frequently display characteristics of conflict, misalignment, and accountability. Lastly, at an individual level, symptoms are dominated by gaps in self-awareness as well as time management issues that manifest themselves in busyness.

Another key difference between medical conditions and business symptoms is that we can test for medical conditions. A good physician listens to a patient's narrative of their symptoms and attempts to distill what is truly happening. Physicians, however, have a powerful set of tools in the form of tests, diagnostics, and procedures that allow them to confirm or disconfirm flaws in a patient's symptomatic and verbal narrative.

There are very few, if any, tests to identify the core issues behind business problems. Balance Sheets, Income Statements, and Cash Flow reports can be useful, but they rarely do more than provide a general direction on where to start looking. Furthermore, financial statements offer precious little insight into behavior-oriented problems at the individual or interpersonal level. And while we can measure that an organization has profitability and turnover issues, our visibility into any deeper understanding often requires a broader set of information that hides far below the surface.

Leaders, consultants, and coaches that work to resolve business problems must rely on a different and more Socratic method to diagnose the core issues behind complex problems. The process of asking questions, pressure-testing assumptions, and carefully examining patterns of behavior is the "business doctor's" method of finding what ails a troubled business. Answers are hidden in the flawed narratives that surround complicated issues and truth is often found beneath the rationalizations we use to comfort our psyches.

> *Which symptoms are you witnessing in your business?*

Let's take this opportunity to better understand these ten most common business symptoms and how they play into the narrative of Diana's story. We will examine them one at a time and observe how Diana begins to fully understand what is happening within her business by examining these symptoms and their impact upon her firm.

# 3

# ACCOUNTABILITY

We've started our list of symptoms with accountability because it's like having a fever– one of the most common medical symptoms. Accountability issues are pervasive and can be symptomatic of countless underlying issues. Much like a fever is often accompanied by chills and body aches, accountability is also very closely related to several other symptoms we will discuss later.

A lack of accountability can lead to frustration. In fact, frustration from accountability issues is not only emotionally charged, but also bi-directional. What that means is that the person who's not delivering an expected result is often as frustrated as the person expecting a result. What's more, accountability issues manifest themselves in more than the frustrations and accusations that decorate the surface. Accountability issues can appear in the form of difficult discussions that have been avoided, improper guidance, unclear communication, competing priorities, and clumsy delegation, among others.

At an *organizational level*, accountability often shows up as unmet objectives or missed goals. Modern data-driven management practices often rely on scorecards and metrics to clearly communicate expectations and evaluate results. That's all well-intentioned, but such impartial structural accountability is profoundly dispassionate, overly mechanized, and frequently troublesome.

The rationale for data-driven management is that you can't improve what you don't measure. And from an HR perspective, structural accountability removes personal prejudice, bias, and interpretation from the judgment of performance in the workplace. What could be more fair? The results are the results, and they speak for themselves.

Accountability can frequently be perceived as unfair or even punitive. Effective organizational accountability is a balancing act built upon trust between those setting the goals and those expected to achieve them.

Managers need to provide adequate resources, proper direction, realistic outcomes, and consistent enforcement. And those being measured need to put forth proper effort, attention to detail, and concern for management directives.

When an organization correctly balances that trust, structural accountability can be quite effective. And when goals are missed, the overall sentiment might be disappointing; but disappointment is generally less impactful than other workplace emotions.

Accountability issues become profoundly more frustrating and emotionally charged when the variables that support a trustful state fall out of balance. And that's when the mood can veer dangerously close to abandonment if you're the one being held accountable, or mutiny if you're the one holding the yardstick.

Knowing this, it's easy to see why accountability issues are so common in business settings. Are goals realistic? Are people putting forth the right effort? Are there enough resources and training to ensure success? Does poor performance have consequences?

We like to massage accountability into binary goals that can be measured discretely without personal bias. But balancing all of the many variables that support such an elegant scheme is a difficult task. As a result, symptomatic accountability issues at the organizational level often have deep roots that are tied to strong underlying feelings about judgment, trust, and fairness.

At an *interpersonal/team level,* symptomatic accountability issues incorporate the same elements of judgment, trust, and fairness as the organizational level. But everything at the interpersonal level is far more intimate– and therefore much more emotionally charged. It's no longer the unfeeling organization assessing your contributions, it is a peer or a co-worker judging your performance. These are people with whom relationships have been established and where a baseline for trust, even if imperfect, is understood.

The interpersonal level is where our relationships keep us from difficult conversations for fear of upsetting a colleague we regularly interact with. Or perhaps our familiarity with co-workers deceives us into assuming our co-workers understand what we "mean" when we delegate a task. Or worse, blind trust quiets our curiosity around conflicting directives and priorities. Whatever the situation, the same benefits that come from a team that works in close cooperation can often lead to accountability issues when we fear upsetting the emotional balance of individual relationships more than the good and unbiased judgment required for true accountability.

Humans are tribal in nature, and it's a painful thought to cull one of our own from the herd and disturb the natural order. Our tribal instincts are deeply embedded in who we are, and we are keenly aware that disrupting the social fabric of any group can initiate a chain reaction of drama and politics that adds to the burden of the task at hand. There is a strong incentive to maintain the status quo within a social group, even if the group is not functioning perfectly.

Perhaps the only thing stronger than our tribal instinct is our survival instinct. When the social fabric of a team breaks down and relationships are stressed, our personal survival instinct takes over. And this is when the proverbial finger starts getting pointed and the CYA *blame game* takes over. Entire bureaucracies and institutions exist to protect, defend, and adjudicate blame.

Blatant finger-pointing is just the most obvious outward symptom of interpersonal accountability issues. At the team level, there are several other less visible ways we camouflage accountability issues within a team or among individuals. Think about politics and gossip— passive-aggressive behaviors that avoid direct confrontation while simultaneously signaling displeasure to the group. These and other dysfunctional behaviors damage team dynamics and interpersonal relationships.

Much like the balance of trust can keep things from going to the extremes at the organizational level, the balance of team dynamics and individual relationships is essential for effective accountability at the interpersonal level. Once again, underlying feelings about judgment, trust and fairness between team members shape interpersonal/team accountability.

At a *personal level,* accountability is a unique symptom with extreme characteristics. Unlike the other two contexts —organizational and interpersonal— personal accountability is somewhat bipolar in nature. Problems with accountability at the personal level are not about being powerless; they can be quite the opposite, more about taking on too much responsibility for a particular outcome. They can be characterized by a failure to understand the broader context of a situation and a lack of recognition or understanding of one's own responsibility. As such, personal accountability tends to be accompanied by profound feelings of either failure or triumph.

At one extreme, we can have a *champion* whose over-inflated estimation of their impact causes them to believe they alone were the reason for a given initiative's success. It's far too common for an individual to have an imbalanced judgment of their importance to a successful outcome, and it's not surprising that our deeply rooted ancestral instincts support and embrace the glorification of champions and heroes. As such, we often empower people to imagine how their efforts were uniquely heroic and important to the cause.

At the opposite end of the spectrum, someone might shoulder the blame for entire groups to protect others who share in a failure. Once again, we have socially accepted this behavior in cultures around the world with stories of martyrdom, atonement, self-sacrifice, and even forgiveness. However magnanimous this self-sacrifice may seem, it's problematic in the business world in that it can send strong signals that co-workers' actions and decisions were less significant to a negative outcome. When people feel insulated from the repercussions of negative outcomes, a new reality exists in which personal responsibility matters less. It's a self-propagating spiral that can have poisonous effects in any culture.

Left unchecked, some symptoms can become so problematic that they initiate additional secondary symptoms. For instance, the slow decay of personal responsibility can lead to new symptoms like lack of agency (to be discussed later) within an organization. It's similar to how ignoring the first indications of an infection can lead to additional symptoms such as fever and chills.

Navigating and correcting accountability issues is a delicate act. At the personal level, it means balancing self-importance and situational awareness, both components of a broader sense of self-awareness. Our view of the world is our own unique perspective, and nothing can change that fact. We are naturally the main character in the narrative each of us creates to establish our importance and make sense of the world around us.

Problems with personal accountability once again spotlight issues of judgment, trust, and fairness. We get into trouble when we trust our self-centered narrative more than the facts around us. This leads to poor judgment that is unfair to everyone, including ourselves.

When we receive feedback that conflicts with our interpretation of reality, we often reject it– it's an affront to our personal narrative and our unique understanding of our place in the world. And while we all know that "feedback is a gift," it can be exceptionally difficult to open. Balanced self-awareness is essential to maintain a proper level of personal accountability.

■ ■ ■

Diana is frustrated with her team members. To her, they aren't holding themselves accountable, and they certainly don't seem to be completing tasks on time or managing the priorities correctly. In fact, issues of accountability with her management team are impossibly entangled with other symptoms, such as missed expectations, alignment, and agency.

A sense of mental exhaustion overcomes Diana as she tries to identify and process all the problems her company is facing. Nothing seems to make sense anymore.

But Diana knows that her clients pay her to solve their most complicated problems. And solving complicated problems requires disciplined thinking; And disciplined thinking is all about thinking through many small issues in a thoughtful manner.

Diana decides to isolate accountability from the other issues plaguing her company. Instead of looking at all her problems at once, she determines that it is more useful to look at her situation through the lens of her most pronounced concern– accountability.

As she begins her analysis, Diana catches herself jumping to conclusions. Her thoughts are buried deep under a layer of emotions and narratives that are preventing any useful analysis of the situation.

Even though Diana is trying her best to be analytical about this process, her frustration is increasing. According to all the advice she has been given and all the books she has read, she has done every-thing right. This whole situation isn't fair, and she doesn't know who she can trust anymore.

And while Diana wants to blame her leaders for all that is going wrong, she knows there is more to this situation.

> *Can you think of a time when you were frustrated, didn't know who you could trust, and just thought the whole situation was unfair?*

Diana's frustration with her people is spilling over into frustra-tion with her own inability to tackle this problem. Nothing seems to make sense.

Diana decides to borrow a trick she learned in her undergrad-uate studies. She calmly finds a notepad and draws a line down the middle of the page. On one side, she writes down everything she knows for sure– the "knowns." The other side is reserved for the things she does not know– the "unknowns."

The "unknowns" take the form of questions she needs to ask if she wishes to understand her accountability issues:

- Do my subordinates have the proper resources to achieve our goals?
- Have our goals become unrealistic?
- Are we avoiding difficult conversations because we don't want to upset employees who we fear might leave?
- Have politics or gossip been increasing?
- Are people starting to point fingers and cast more blame?
- Do we have any champions or martyrs emerging?

> *Is your organization plagued with gossip and politics?*
> *Is blame more prevalent than ownership of problems?*
> *Who are the champions or martyrs in your company?*

It doesn't take long for Diana to realize that her inability to pinpoint her firm's accountability issues is a direct result of questions she had failed to ask.

When faced with the answers to these questions, Diana realizes that the stress on resources has doubled in recent months and that few people have the time to deal with the multitude of issues her organization is facing. This increased stress created the first wave of people leaving the organization, which only made problems worse.

Accordingly, many goals were no longer realistic and tribal rifts began forming between management and the consulting staff. This used to be a high-performing organization with tremendous harmony between all levels of employees. Currently, though, fingers are being pointed right and left. Employees bargaining for wage increases sound like champions while some of Diana's most loyal managers are sounding more like martyrs. People seem to be picking sides with feelings of betrayal and mutiny simmering below the surface.

At this point, Diana may not have a "perfect" understanding of the entire situation, but she does have a much better picture of what is going on. And all of this was achieved by asking a few questions from a slightly different perspective.

The remaining questions that Diana may have trouble asking herself are regarding her own self-awareness:

- Did she minimize her importance and situational awareness while this pot boiled over?
- How might she be accountable for what is going on within her organization?

Just like a doctor evaluates a patient's narrative and symptoms to arrive at a correct diagnosis, a wise business leader must do the same. In this case, though, the leader is not a dispassionate third-party evaluating the narrative and symptoms like the doctor. The leader is playing an active and emotionally involved role in the story. This is why advisors and consultants can often see a problem more clearly than the parties involved in any situation.

However, the discipline to diagnose a business problem correctly does NOT require a third-party. It is just easier, and sometimes faster, when an outsider is asking the questions.

# 4

## AGENCY

Possessing agency and controlling your own destiny is a wonderful and powerful place to be. It takes hard work and discipline as evidenced by both Stoic and Eastern Buddhist philosophies. Stoic philosophers such as Socrates, Marcus Aurelias, and Epictetus provided clarity around the importance of devoting time to only that which we can control and not upon that which we do not control.

When we are diagnosing business problems, the dysfunctional symptom we observe is a lack of agency. Dysfunction is exactly why agency, or lack thereof, is the less impressive younger sibling to accountability. The two are closely related, but agency is less sophisticated, more irrational, and far more disappointing. People and teams that lack accountability may be frustrating but any person, team or organization, that exhibits a lack of agency raises our level of contempt because of their weak and feckless behavior.

Perhaps the best place to start examining agency is at the *personal level*. This is because of the obvious nature in how it presents itself as a symptom. In many situations, agency will have an individual who plays the part of a victim. It is easy to spot because we like to embellish our flawed narratives in ways that emphasize our status as either a hero or a victim. When we craft narratives to explain the world around us, we tend to subconsciously minimize our flaws and amplify the challenges we face. Our grand narratives include insurmountable odds and best efforts to fight the unwinnable, good fight. The more we tell these stories to ourselves and others, the more we actually buy into carefully created false narratives that attempt to paint us as a hero but reveal us as a victim.

The acid test for whether someone has truly lost their agency and is operating with a victim mentality is to evaluate their locus of control (Rotter, 1954). This important psychological concept is the degree to which you believe you control your destiny as opposed to external forces having a greater influence over the events in your life. Put simply, you either believe your actions determine your future or that other people's actions (or outside influences) determine your fate. If you have an internal locus of control, you believe you are the primary influencer of your future. If you have an external locus of control, the world happens to you. People with an external locus of control abdicate their personal responsibility and agency in several ways.

The most common influencer of declining personal agency is fear. Individuals will sacrifice their agency in making decisions because they fear making the wrong decision. This fear leads people into the common trap of "analysis paralysis" where more information in support of a more perfect decision is always on the immediate horizon. Fears of being wrong or not finding the ideal solution may come from punitive management practices, perfectionist tendencies, or even a fear of success. However misguided, the rationalization that no decision is better than a wrong decision is a common justification for people who have lost their agency. Regardless of the rationale, a lack of agency at the personal level is a self-inflicted limitation.

Perhaps the most interesting way in which individuals constrain their agency is through habit. We can have good habits and bad habits; but regardless of their bias, habits have a mesmerizing influence on our agency. Habits fool us into limiting our available options and relinquishing a portion of our agency, while simultaneously comforting us, just like the story we enjoyed hearing repeatedly as children.

Habits do not exist "outside the box" where we know a wider range of creative options exist. The "box" represents the sum of the limitations we believe to exist on our available options at any given moment. These limitations are a culmination of our assumptions, biases, fears, imagination, and perceived understanding of unwritten rules we readily obey. And while these limitations can be imagined or real, they are all very tangible in the restrictive impact they have on our ability to evaluate possible options. The most fascinating aspect of habits and the proverbial "box" is that we are in total control of creating the very limitations we allow to govern our behavior.

There are countless ways in which we unwittingly invent narratives, amplify fears and construct limitations to avoid the responsibility that comes with decision making. Symptomatically, individuals unknowingly relinquish their agency like they subconsciously bite their fingernails– oblivious to how conspicuous this involuntary behavior is to the casual observer.

At the *interpersonal/ team level,* agency is a bit more complicated because it involves a shared sense of disempowerment. This concept is quite amazing when you consider how difficult it is to persuade any group of people to collectively hold the same belief.

However, when you study leadership, you can see how the simplest and most popular leadership style makes this possible. Leadership by division, a method we learn in our youth, is a powerful and caustic leadership technique that splits groups into binary elements– us and them. In this leadership paradigm *we* are right, and *they* are wrong. By demonizing another group, we not only unify on a common enemy, but we also feed into a familiar external locus of control. When framed this way, our problems are because of *them*. Our lack of results is because of *them*. Our options are limited because of *them*. It doesn't even matter who *they* are… all that matters is that *they* are not us. It doesn't take long to evaluate historical events and the world around us to realize that this is a profoundly popular and powerful leadership tactic. Unfortunately, leadership by division leaves deep scars and is quite acrimonious and reprehensible in nature.

This paradigm fits well into our tribal nature and feeds victimization narratives we tend to favor. Making the group narrative even more seductive is the fact that it is far more acceptable to have lost your agency as a member of an oppressed group than if you were individually singled out. Blame is unquestioned when you are victimized as part of a group- *they* are to blame!

The other combustible element that is accelerated when we divide ourselves into tribal camps is groupthink. Groupthink is a psychological phenomenon that happens when the desire for conformity within a group results in irrational or dysfunctional decisions. Group members tend to agree with these decisions at all costs in order to maintain a unified coalition. A heightened attention to harmony allows decisions to be made without any critical analysis. This group-imposed echo chamber can further exacerbate feelings of victimization and reduce the collective agency of the group.

Just as group dynamics can further increase feelings of victimization, they can also increase fear. Fear is a powerful behavioral influence within groups and a compelling factor in diminishing agency. At a team level, individuals may fear voicing new ideas because they risk lowering their social status through ridicule, or worse, expulsion from the group. Letting someone else take the risk for making a decision is a prudent political play in these situations.

However, an even more cautious play is to maintain group harmony by suggesting that nobody in the group can make this decision because we don't yet have sufficient information. This crafty insertion of "analysis paralysis" into the mix can raise your social status and buy time for the group to coalesce around any new idea in a less risky manner. The inherent flaw is that there is always additional information to be found and there is always a more optimal solution. The net result is a group that has lost its agency because acceptance and status within the group have become more important than actual progress.

Micromanagement is perhaps the most comical of all interpersonal agency killers. There are many reasons why someone might micromanage their team, but regardless of the reason, it is truly amazing how one person's desire for control can crush the agency of entire teams.

Micromanagement is funny because it requires so much effort and it universally results in decreased agency for the people being managed. The only surefire results of this short-sighted and counterproductive management technique are more work for the manager and less engaged and empowered employees.

The fascinating part of agency is that people are completely fine losing their agency if they are doing it on their own terms. However, when someone else restricts their agency, people resist and fight back. This is not only why micromanagement receives such a visceral negative response, it is also why smaller and less noticeable constraints on agency also elicit strong negative reactions.

A subtle and more common form of mismanagement is when one person recommends that another person *should* do something. The small addition of the words like *should* or *need* into a recommendation has a disproportionate impact upon an individual's reaction. When we suggest that someone else *needs* to do something, we may be thinking we are helping them, but we are subtly removing their choice and replacing it with a singular directive. Good mentors and coaches know that a more productive way to approach this dialogue is to suggest ideas for someone to consider. Asking someone to consider an option protects their ability to choose and increases agency as well as personal responsibility.

Group dynamics closely mimic the personal dynamics in how agency is diminished. The struggles of control, acceptance, and fear that happen within groups are similar to the personal conflicts of responsibility, limitations, and fear that constantly battle for control within our psyches.

The ways in which we structurally restrict agency at the *organizational level* are strangely well-documented and profoundly frustrating. In the spirit of consistency and quality, we establish standards, regulations, and policies to ensure that our products, services, and management practices align with organizational responsibilities. When rules are implemented correctly, they also serve the purpose of benevolently supporting proper judgment, stakeholder trust and fairness for all involved.

However well-intentioned, rules and regulations always have unexpected consequences. Furthermore, when these unintended consequences are identified, organizations rarely curtail their flawed origins. Instead, organizations respond by adding more rules and regulations to fix the old ones. This process surreptitiously creates a patchwork quilt of intertwined conflictions and stifling complexity.

As sophisticated as we are, humans don't particularly like complexity. We have a bias toward simplicity. We like to explain the world to ourselves with narratives that have comfortable storylines and predictable outcomes. Complex stories are not as appealing as simple anecdotes and analogies. It is no wonder that sound bites, taglines and catchphrases are as effective as they are. Our preference for simplicity is why great leaders are praised for distilling complex messages into powerful narratives that still capture the original intent and purpose.

When complexity persists and grows within an organization, people eventually stop fighting the bureaucracy and surrender portions of their agency to the mountains of red tape. There is a boundary of bureaucratic regulation that gains almost human characteristics when it is crossed. You can often recognize when organizations have crossed that threshold because "the system" becomes an antagonist in the narratives of employees that have lost some degree, if not all, of their agency. The "system" has an almost supernatural authority to wrestle control from able bodied employees and render them powerless.

Bureaucracies can be maddening because they frequently elevate the importance of arcane historical events above future-focused thinking based on current conditions. The "system" can manifest itself in the form of convoluted HR policies, legacy computer systems, government regulation or standardized procedures. Whatever form it takes, the "system" comes to life and drives employees, customers, and leadership to the edges of sanity.

Eventually, organizational inefficiencies driven by years of fealty to unending corporate bureaucracy, can establish a forceful presence within an organization's culture. The longer we loyally obey the limitations imposed by structural bureaucracy the more forcefully it cements its authority upon the organization.

■ ■ ■

On the surface, Diana's management team seems to have lost their agency regarding the turnover and retention issues. While her leaders are well aware of the problems, their paralysis outlines a lack of understanding of the situation and a fear of what to do next.

> *Can you think of a time when your team was paralyzed with indecision and inaction?*

Having been a consultant for many years, Diana knows that complex issues require disciplined thinking. She considers how she can isolate her situation through the lens of agency and quickly arrives at a few questions to ask:

- What are employees saying in exit interviews?
- What ideas do her managers have to retain employees?
- What reasons are her managers giving her for their indecision and inaction regarding retention issues?
- Are her leaders using victim language?

The answers to these questions reveal a management team that feels victimized and helpless. All Diana hears is a chorus of knee-jerk reactions that the consultants need to be paid more money. Diana has been here before and knows that bumps in pay are a temporary fix. Additionally, she is frustrated because the new incentive program should allow for increased income for her consulting staff.

Diana wonders why her leaders seem to be throwing up their arms defeated by cries for increased pay. She realizes that her true problem is much deeper than the symptoms of paralysis, indecision, or a lack of agency. Why would leaders who have performed well in the past, suddenly display such feckless behavior?

She knows she must dig further to reveal some less obvious questions that might be useful to further assess the situation from the context of agency:

- Are there groups/factions developing where problems are being blamed on *them*?

- Are there unintended consequences of the new incentive program?
- Are there any policies and procedures that are constraining her team's ability to deal with changing market conditions?
- Is her leadership team micromanaging their employees?
- Why do some employees feel the agency to leave while others exercise the agency to negotiate?
- Is leaving or negotiating the only way for employees to win back their agency?

As Diana digs deeper into the situation, she discovers that the incentive program may have created some unintended consequences. Her company was growing at a rapid pace and the goal of the new program was to balance out the workload and reward teams that were shouldering more of the burden as the company grew. Much of her management team was uncomfortable with growth focused incentives as they were more aligned with the core environmental mission of the organization.

It turns out that one manager, David, really enjoyed the challenge of implementing the new incentive program. Because Diana's management team was already working long hours, many of them were thrilled to abdicate their involvement in the rollout of the new program. Considering this power vacuum, David took charge and handled all aspects of the implementation. David was newer to the organization and most of his co-workers thought that he was using the initiative to make a name for himself. His peers, many of whom were already working long hours, were happy to oblige and Diana was thrilled to see one of her newer managers show such initiative.

The remaining managers selfishly supported David as his efforts relieved much of the burden the new program would place on them. In retrospect, it does not seem as though many of the employees truly understood the intentions of the new program.

Exit interviews suggested that employees did not like the new numbers-oriented focus of the company that seemed to stray from the core environmental mission that attracted them to Diana's company in the first place.

Other employees observed how their contributions made significant impacts to the numbers within the new incentive program. In some cases, these employees were emboldened to capitalize on the perceived value of their newly highlighted contributions.

As she learns more, Diana realizes that the rift that was developing was not necessarily between management and staff; it was developing between those who felt connected to the shared environmental mission and those that were more motivated by individual accolades and benefits. Since most of her management team had been with her for many years, they were naturally the group that was most connected to the mission. They were all there in the beginning when good salaries and work-life balance was not part of the equation. Diana's long-time consultants are staying with her for the moment, but there is growing concern that Diana is straying from the powerful mission that originally bound them all together.

> *Do your employees view your management metrics as being aligned with your company mission and vision?*

Everything was going so well, and now Diana is even more distraught about the changes going on in her organization. At the same time, something amazing is happening. The sleepless nights she was having just a few days ago are subsiding. As she learns more about the problems within her organization, Diana's perspective of the narrative is changing. She has greater clarity, and the improved understanding helps her think through the next set of questions she needs to ask. Instead of lying awake in bed at night, she now falls asleep exhausted, but wakes with new thoughts and ideas on what to do next. Diana is learning that curiosity is one of the strongest tools any leader brings to the job.

The one thing that still troubles Diana is her role in everything that is happening. Why has she been so distanced from all of this? Has she lost some of her agency in running the business as she let go of the reins? Diana knows she needs to get involved, but she still doesn't know what she needs to do or why she would need to do it. Perhaps some of the most important questions that remain can only be answered by Diana.

# 5

## EXPECTATIONS

Understanding business problems can be just as difficult as diagnosing medical conditions. This is why good business consultants and advisors have many years of experience, just like becoming a doctor requires many years of schooling. Doctors often face situations where many symptoms are present and some of them are strikingly similar. Consider medical symptoms such as fever and chills. These are distinctly different symptoms, but they are closely related and often found in tandem. In many ways, we never think to distinguish the two from one another.

This analogy is a great way to understand the relationship between accountability and expectations; two symptoms that are closely related and often found together. Just as a fever may induce chills, missed expectations may also trigger issues with accountability. It would be nice if things were that simple, but alas, the symbiotic nature of accountability and expectations is far more complex. What allows us to distinguish each of these symptoms and see them independently is a matter of perspective. Put simply, accountability is for the person doing the work whereas expectations are for the person receiving or evaluating the work. Who sets those expectations and how they are understood is where expectation management gets interesting.

Accountability, as we learned earlier, is all about taking responsibility for results. What is important is that those results are at the endpoints of any project, process, or objective. And those endpoints are always evaluated in the past. Expectation management is a bit more complex. Expectation management also includes additional information such as the method in which a result is achieved, or the experience people have in the process of completing an objective. Additionally, expectations can be evaluated before, during and after an outcome is reported.

As a result, two factors really distinguish accountability from expectations - time and method.

| Before | ⇨ | Expectation |
| During | ⇨ | Experience |
| After  | ⇨ | Opinion |

When we combine both time and method, we begin to see a clearer picture of how expectations differ from results. We have expectations before any project is started, purchase is made, or event commences. While we use any product or engage in any service, we have experiences that we compare to our original expectations. And then, upon concluding any process or purchase we can reflect and form opinions about our experience and how that compared to what we anticipated.

It may now be easier to see how our expectations evolve over time, but we have yet to address how our expectations are originally set. Our expectations are formed through narratives we tell ourselves or infer from others. Those same narratives are also powerfully influenced by convenient shared histories such as reputation, organizational culture, and lore. Regardless of their origin, expectations are all about the accuracy of the narrative we have in our mind across a continuum of time.

One of the most frequent nuggets of business advice when dealing with other people is to set expectations properly. Hence, it makes perfect sense to start our analysis at an *interpersonal level*. When we set expectations, we are part storyteller, part fortune teller, and part historian; weaving the future, present and past into a cohesive narrative. We often start by finding common ground and getting agreement on where we are today. In support of that process, we may even tell a story of how we got to where we are today to further develop the narrative arc. Facts and figures are inserted into our stories like signs along a roadway– discrete markers that affirm our situation and comfort our logical sensibilities.

Having grounded our story in both the past and present we can now begin to extrapolate our thoughts to a better, brighter, or different future. The success of the "expectation setter" improves when they can inspire the listener with emotional vignettes that engage our more creative sentiments.

Any good story is interpreted in three ways: logically, emotionally, and harmoniously. Consider listening to music in stereo. The logical component of the story is heard by your left ear. The emotional perspective of the story is heard by your right ear. If we only listened to one channel at a time, we might like both stories. However, when we listen to both at the same time, the combined stereo production only sounds good if they are in synchronous harmony. A well-constructed "harmonized" narrative binds the facts and figures that satisfy our logical brain with the emotional content that our creative mind craves. Setting expectations properly is a delicate balance of harmonizing the logical and creative narratives our brains interpret.

The skill in setting expectations does not stop with a properly harmonized narrative. Complicating this process further is the fact that the storyteller has precious little control over how that message is received, perceived, or realized in another person's mind.

The true skill in setting expectations is how to paint a picture of the future in a manner that has consistent messaging from the painter's intent through to the observer's perception.

Consider a general that orders troops to travel to a remote village to deal with complaints. Having just put down an uprising of guerillas in this area, the general is keen to repair relations with the local villagers. The general figures that water pipelines need to be fixed or electricity needs to be restored before the villagers will be happy again. He instructs one of his captains to quiet their complaints. The captain, having spent the last several months fighting in this area, does not hear this order with the same intent in which it was given. The complaints are quieted, but many villagers are manhandled and upset in the process. The general is furious, because his intent was misconstrued, and the captain has just minted the next set of guerillas. This tragic misunderstanding is a failure to properly communicate the "commander's intent;" a topic that is discussed in the military because of the extreme consequences that can occur when communications are unclear. Understandably, modern militaries have learned to be precise in how they describe their "rules of engagement" in order to prevent such tragedies and preserve the "commander's intent."

In the business world, however, the consequences are less extreme and the skill in describing intent is far less developed. Unrecognized assumptions run rampant within organizations and are the source of many expectation management issues. When we think of Hollywood movie narratives, assumptions neatly fill the moments where we suspend disbelief and accept the premise of time travel or zombies. This is convenient when we are entertaining ourselves, but exceptionally counter-productive when we are attempting to set realistic expectations.

Expectation setting is an involved process that requires time and effort. And at an interpersonal level, employees and managers rarely invest the time necessary to produce the tight storyline required to properly set expectations. All too often, an employee can meet all their numerical objectives and still fall short of a more subjective measure that influences what was expected of them. A failure to fully outline and understand the full spectrum of expectations is what makes this such a profoundly frustrating and common business symptom.

The regularity of this source of frustration lends itself to yet another common, yet misleading, business maxim: setting expectations low so you know you can exceed them. The flaw with this advice is that it temporarily allows someone to exceed expectations, but it simultaneously highlights a narrative that is clearly inaccurate. Those inconsistencies in the story tend to degrade trust and force a guaranteed "adjustment factor" on all future narratives and expectations set by the individual using this flawed maxim as a guide. And since we know that it is already very difficult to form narratives that are received as clearly as they are crafted, the burden becomes even more onerous when we must also deal with an adjustment factor.

As stated earlier, managing expectations is all about maintaining the accuracy of a narrative over time. And when additional stakeholders are involved, the accuracy of the narrative must be consistent for all affected parties.

Perhaps the best advice for anyone wishing to manage expectations well is to keep narratives simple and clean. Unfortunately, this is harder to do than it would seem. Henry David Thoreau said it best: "Not that the story need be long, but it will take a long while to make it short." Business problems love the camouflage that is embedded in long explanations and intricate details that a tidy narrative fails to offer.

The narratives we use to set expectations fall apart when the fidelity of a story falls apart. If there is no harmony between logical track and the emotional track, the story falls apart. If there is no reliability between the message sent and the message received, the story falls apart. If anticipated results and actual outcomes differ greatly, the story falls apart. If the path to the outcome varies greatly from the planned route, the story falls apart. And when the story falls apart, it is a guarantee that expectations set do not align with obligations met.

It may seem counterintuitive to address expectation management symptoms at an *individual level,* but it is quite important. We are often our own worst enemies when it comes to creating and interpreting narratives. And since narratives are an essential component of expectation setting, we tend to unwittingly affect that process.

Our problems start with the fact that we do not like gaps in our stories. Gaps destroy narratives and narratives are what we use to make sense of the world around us. Whenever there is a gap, we feel compelled to fill the void to make order out of chaos. This urge is exceptionally strong and is powered by one of our most rebellious human capabilities, our imagination.

What is fascinating about our imagination is that it will always take you to an extreme outcome. Imaginations love fantastical stories with unicorns and rainbows or the catastrophes where everything imaginable goes wrong. Our imaginations never seek the reasonable outcome that is rationally grounded and centered in common sense.

Even small gaps in a given narrative can be the crack through which imagination does its dirty work. Like water seeping through a wall, imagination slowly destroys narratives and distances expectations far away from a productive reality. The corrosive power of an imagination run wild can skew expectations wildly for anyone trying to set or meet an expectation.

There is a singular word that encompasses expectations at an *organizational level:* quality.

We attribute quality to things for which we have high expectations in the future, enjoy great performance in the present and have fond recollections of the past. Quality is a characteristic that endures over time. Quality is not a characteristic you occasionally display; quality requires consistent performance over a continuum of time.

And while quality can be attributed to individuals, we know that it is more commonly attributed to products, services, and organizations. Quality is embedded into the brand essence of a product, the memorable experience of services and the legend of organizations. Quality is a powerful element of the narratives that accompany the output and the experiences that organizations provide.

Quality is typically put into question when narratives and expectations are at odds with results. When your package has not arrived by 10am, your pizza is not delivered with the correct toppings, or your car strands you on the road, the supporting narratives that define expectations for an organization also break down.

And while strong and coherent narratives help organizations set and maintain their quality reputation, there is a small detail that is often overlooked. Quality is not a one-dimensional characteristic. Quality comes in two distinctly different flavors: product quality and process quality.

Product quality focuses on the result of efforts that organizations put into their products, services, or deliverables. A car can be a quality product. A consulting report can be a quality product. A delicious pastry can be a quality product.

The aspect of quality that is most often overlooked is process quality. As Joe Pine and Jim Gilmore suggest in *The Experience Economy,* one of the most profound ways that an organization can differentiate their products and/or services is through the experience they provide. Great examples of this are Disney theme parks, American Girl doll stores, and Starbucks coffee shops.

Few items are as commoditized as a cup of coffee. Yet Starbucks commands a premium price and a loyal following that cannot be justified on taste alone. Starbucks pays close attention to the experience that is provided for their customers. The music, the décor, the store locations, the signature cups, and even the fact that there is a line to wait for your coffee are all important elements of the total experience provided for a Starbucks customer. It all works for Starbucks because a premium priced coffee product should not only taste great, but it should also feel great.

But much like the analogy of listening to a story in stereo (logic, emotion, and harmony), quality has a similar interdependency between process quality and product quality. A great product delivered in a careless and lazy manner loses much of its quality luster. A terrible product delivered elegantly appears to be a ruse. However, when the perceived quality of a product is in harmony with the way it is delivered… expectations of quality can grow and thrive.

Managing organizational expectations is all about the coherence between product and process quality. It is not enough for the final product to be good. The experience of getting to the final product must also be good.

Organizational expectations are always measured by the lower of the two components between product and process quality. So, when our expectations match closely with our experiences of both product and process quality, we can safely form a quality opinion of the organization with whom we are dealing.

■ ■ ■

Diana still has grave concerns about her team and the health of her business, but she is waking up each morning with a determination to understand what ails the company she loves. Seeking truth and clarity is fueling much of her renewed energy, but disappointment from missed expectations is a crushing pressure that saps away her passion by the end of each day. She has been waking up each morning with a renewed interest in learning more, but she fears that what she is doing is unsustainable. What if she wakes up tomorrow and the desire to persist and understand her plight is no longer there?

> *Has the daily grind ever worn you down to the point where you imagine if it is time to give up?*

Putting these concerns aside, Diana presses on and contemplates how her ideas and directives have become so fractured within her team. She used to be great at communicating the strong mission of her environmental consulting firm.

Diana begins by asking herself a series of questions:

- What has changed?
- Why are people interpreting her thoughts in such different ways?
- What did I miss when I was speaking with each of these individuals?

It is at this point that Diana has her first revelation of the day. She realizes she is not asking questions of her team. Diana is having an entire Socratic dialogue with herself. And through this self-reflection she recognizes the following:

- The incentive system is complex, and it allows people to get lost in the details.
- There were far too many gaps in what she told people. They used their imaginations to fill in those gaps and bias their conclusions.

- She knew that everyone interprets information differently, so she adjusted her narrative to have it resonate with each person for maximum impact. However, her message needed to be heard in "stereo." The logical explanation of the incentive system does not work without connecting it to the emotional narrative that binds her employees to the broader mission.

- The incentive program and the metrics behind it made her desire for growth appear to be 100% financially motivated. In reality, all she wanted was a healthy and growing business that could accelerate the social impact of the company's core mission.

> ### *When do you make time to ask yourself questions?*

It is then when Diana has a second and more terrifying revelation. Who else does she need to be speaking with? Diana realizes that if she is not happy… perhaps her customers are also not happy.

Diana carefully considers which clients to contact and what she should ask them. She decides to contact three clients that might offer different perspectives. The first client Diana speaks with is one of her oldest and dearest clients. This client has been with Diana since the beginning and generally works with the more established consultants. As usual, the conversation is friendly, honest, and thoroughly enjoyable. However, during the discussion, her client does indicate that some of her staff just seem to be a bit more tired and stressed than normal. Diana receives no indication as to why… just the notion that her team seems a bit "off their game."

Armed with this information, Diana decides to connect with a newer client that has just started doing business with her firm. This firm is working closely with David, the employee who has been enthusiastically leading the efforts to roll out the new incentive plan. This client is amazed at the results his firm is receiving. After several minutes of listening to detailed reports of how much carbon emissions have decreased and energy efficiency has been increased, even Diana is impressed. But before she can enjoy these successes, the client utters a phrase that always gives pause— *"but while I have you on the phone…"*

In the subsequent discussion Diana's client reveals that results have been great, but the experience of working with David is not always pleasant. David can often be too curt and direct with his communication and rarely explains what was done, why it was done, or how they can learn to do things better themselves. David is all about results and that is not what they had come to expect through the sales process. An embarrassed Diana acknowledges the deficiency and promises to address the situation promptly.

This feedback makes Diana change who she speaks with next. The client she decides to speak with has engaged her firm for the single largest project in the history of her company. Originally, she did not want to probe into this project for fear of stirring the pot and putting the project at risk. Now, however, she realizes that not having this discussion is likely a greater risk. Diana makes the strategic decision to speak with her client's project manager rather than the General Manager sponsoring the project. If there is a problem, Diana knows she must find it first.

In her discussion, the client's project manager reveals that different teams within Diana's organization do not know what the other teams from her own firm are doing. The project manager has rationalized that this is most likely due to the tremendous scope of this undertaking, but Diana knows better. If left unattended, this issue could impact the project and affect an important relationship for her firm. As Diana probes deeper, she finds that tribal rifts observed inside the office also exist outside the office. Some individuals are seeking personal glory and others are trying to salvage the purity of the firm's original mission.

Diana now realizes that her firm may still be delivering results for clients, but the way those results are achieved is not up to her personal standards and certainly not to her clients' expectations. The quality of her firm's work is declining, and it is only a matter of time before opinions start to change and the reputation she has worked ten years to build is damaged.

And while the discovery of quality issues with clients are concerning, Diana is empowered by her first revelation of the day. The answers she seeks, appear to be close to home and within reach.

# 6

# ALIGNMENT

Misalignment is, perhaps, one of the more perplexing symptoms that a business can exhibit. The rationale for this is that misalignment is often grossly apparent to an outsider well before it is recognized by those who are operating out of alignment.

Alignment is not just as simple as setting and communicating a direction. In actuality, communicating and setting direction is more related to setting expectations than it is to alignment. Alignment is something different. Alignment is mostly about **maintaining** that direction for teams of people and entire organizations. Maintaining alignment can be a rather sloppy process because the moving parts –individual people– all need to be operating with a similar understanding of the destination and the path forward.

When you consider that there are entire sports (ballroom dance, figure skating pairs, synchronized swimming, etc.) that are dedicated to perfecting the coordination and alignment between just two people, you can imagine the enormity of the task at hand for a business that may have hundreds, or thousands of people involved.

Years ago, maps disappeared from the glove compartments of cars and are now only found in pirate movies. They were replaced by one of our most treasured modern conveniences– the navigation system. These modern technological marvels are so much better than maps because of one simple difference– feedback! A navigation system can tell you where you are. A map does not. Armed with real-time satellite feedback, every wrong turn, missed exit, or construction zone allows for a recalculation and immediate corrective action.

For businesses to stay in alignment, they require **feedback** just like our cars require GPS location data to keep us on course. Misalignment happens in business when we don't seek feedback, we can't obtain feedback, or we do not fully understand the feedback we are receiving.

It may seem foolish to think about alignment at an *individual level*, but it is actually quite important. The reason for this is because individuals are the most elemental building block of organizational alignment. Furthermore, when we investigate how individuals receive feedback it is important to establish the fact that people prefer affirming feedback and tend to reject corrective feedback. Put simply, we like praise and we hate criticism.

Think of this from a medical perspective. When we are in great shape, we are eager to hear about our blood pressure, weight, and cholesterol levels. But when we are not in good shape, we are content to let our scale collect dust and allow more time to lapse between visits to the doctor.

When we lack —or reject— the feedback that allows us to correct our path forward, small mistakes tend to compound on one another and lead us astray. This is how we get lost on car trips, get out of shape over time and definitely how teams and organizations get out of alignment.

Any experienced carpenter will be able to tell a story about how a small and imperceptible measuring mistake propagated several times turned into a horrific problem. Small changes slowly add up and are rarely noticed until a critical component does not fit, typically at a crucial moment. For a carpenter, measurement is a conscious decision to seek feedback and accept the results regardless if they are good or bad.

As individuals, our ability to intentionally seek and accept both affirming and corrective feedback is what drives us forward in productive ways that are aligned with our goals.

In business, and in life, feedback is either given or received based on our interactions with other people. And that is exactly why we need to look at the *interpersonal* aspects of alignment next. The complexity of interpersonal alignment is not necessarily how we receive feedback, but the impediments that keep us from providing important feedback to others.

In my experiences, there are two main factors that determine how we share feedback with other people: how we feel about the other person and how we feel about ourselves in the relationship. The diagram below can help us understand the complex interpersonal dynamics at play.

DISGUST/CONTEMPT — INFATUATION/ADMIRATION

DOMINANT — DEPENDENT

Feelings About Yourself — In the Relationship

Your Feelings About the Other Person — In the Relationship

As with any analysis of this nature, it is often useful to look at extreme conditions before we ratchet back our focus to a more moderate scenario. The reason why this is useful is because it sets the boundaries of a continuum that exists across our relationships with others. It might be easier and cleaner to create boxes and categories of relationship types, but that would assume relationships are static in nature. We all know that relationships constantly evolve so it is important to evaluate their impact on the feedback we provide with a more dynamic model.

In this more dynamic model, the x-axis represents how we feel about the other person. At one extreme it can be disgust or contempt. At the opposite end of the spectrum, it can be infatuation or admiration. The y-axis represents how we feel about ourselves within that relationship. The extremes for this sentiment cover the range from feelings of dependence to feelings of dominance. When we evaluate our relationships under these extreme situations, the impact on the feedback we provide is quite predictable.

In the lower left quadrant, when we feel dependent upon someone and we truly despise them, we tend to be very quiet. Our relationship with that person is one of compliance and our feedback is quite minimal. We will likely be polite and will generally comment only when an inquiry is made of us.

In the upper left quadrant, when we feel strong and are in a dominant position, but we simultaneously have contempt for someone, we tend to avoid interaction with them. That avoidance is an implicit form of negative feedback. Additionally, when feedback is provided in these extreme conditions, it is rarely –if ever– positive.

In the upper right, we have situations where we are in charge and we allow ourselves to be charmed by the idea of a superstar protégé that can share the burden and make our lives easier. We are always looking for the next "prodigy" and when we find someone who might fit the bill, we often envision them to be more than what they may actually be. Infatuations such as this often blind us to flaws in character and gaps in capability. In this state, a clouded view of reality distorts our perspective and prevents us from processing feedback that would challenge the status of our protégé. As such, we tend to provide overwhelming affirmations and positive feedback to these individuals.

The lower right quadrant is the home of heroes and idols. When we feel more dependent in a relationship it is easy to become enchanted by the idea of a hero who can rescue us. It is rare for people to do anything but heap praise upon their heroes. In fact, the overwhelming degree of affirmation without any corrective feedback is often the process that feeds a hero's hubris and leads to their downfall.

As you may have noticed, a pattern has emerged at the extremes. There are far fewer circumstances where we provide corrective advice compared to the situations where we provide affirming praise. Put simply, we avoid difficult discussions. This imbalance and lack of corrective feedback is a strong impediment to any efforts to retain or regain alignment between two individuals.

As we back off the extremes, it is useful to consider the very center of the matrix. Even though both parties may not feel the same way about themselves or the other person in a relationship, the center is a healthy and productive place for the person providing feedback. Feedback emanating from a person who is in this "sweet spot" will tend to be more respectful, balanced, and clear-eyed. In these situations, the urge to pile on praise or criticism is subdued in favor of a more authentic communication that is perceived as genuine and fair.

However, even feedback originating from a person who is in the "sweet spot" can be troublesome. It is established science that any corrective feedback is best received when it is delivered in a ratio of at least 5 affirming statements to every 1 corrective statement

(Gottman, 1993). Maintaining this balance over time is difficult and time consuming and is only practiced regularly by the very best coaches, managers, and leaders.

As you can see, the nature of a relationship -how we feel about ourselves and others in that relationship- determines whether we stay silent, criticize, or praise our colleagues. Further adding to the challenge of providing feedback is the necessity to carefully manage the balance of feedback to a more efficacious 5:1 positivity ratio.

*Organizational alignment* is a process that is more akin to the effort a sheepdog exerts to guide the flock toward their destination. There are many times when there is confusion within the flock, some sheep stray; and various sub-groups require different levels of attention. The skill that a trained herding dog exhibits in alertly reacting to the auditory and visual cues emanating from the sheep is truly something to behold. A skilled leader, much like the sheepdog, must also be vigilant, responsive, and relentless. Unlike the sheep-dog, though, a business leader does not enjoy the luxury of any immediate visual or auditory cues that misalignment is taking place.

Monitoring the activity of an organization like a sheepdog, however, is not the answer. When people are monitored too closely, complaints of micromanagement and mistrust are more disruptive than the benefit gained from swift corrective feedback. Instead, organizations typically empower people by creating incentives to provide the proper rationale for individuals to align with corporate goals and overall objectives.

Here is where the concept of "commander's intent" comes into play again. We can consider ourselves in tight alignment when there is harmony between our goals (outcomes) and our overall objec-tive (intent). However, when there is a gap between outcomes and intents, we get out of alignment in ways that are often gradual and imperceptible.

The problem with incentives is that they are easy to create for outcomes and far more difficult to craft for proper intent. Outcomes have the convenience of usually being easy to measure. The intent of an objective can be far more difficult, if not impossible, to measure. As a result, most incentive programs are geared more toward goals whereas the intent is left to corporate guidelines, policies, and values. Unfortunately, most performance recognition programs increasingly favor achievement of goals over adherence to corporate values. This one-dimensional feedback mechanism for incentivizing employee behavior unwittingly creates the very structures that undermine the alignment of outcomes and intent.

Another insidious way we get out of alignment is by creating competing incentives. Companies have far greater needs than the sheep in our example. Organizations deal with many clients, a multitude of business objectives, and employee retention issues to name a few of the many challenges businesses face. As such, employees are often operating under several incentive programs at any given time. It is a rare occurrence to find an organization whose incentive programs do not contain confusing intersections and unintentional conflicts.

How we receive and give feedback is an essential component of maintaining alignment within a business. It is clear that the complexities of human nature and competing business priorities make alignment a very delicate state to maintain. Accordingly, misalignment is an exceptionally common business symptom.

■ ■ ■

Diana has always considered herself a strong communicator with an unwavering belief in the core mission of her environmental consulting firm. Her "True North" story, that is retold at every company meeting, was the guide she expected to align and focus her team on the firm's common objectives. In ten years, the story hasn't changed, further confounding Diana at how her team has splintered into so many different groups with varied interpretations.

As Diana contemplates her firm's troubles, her attention quickly shifts to David; the rising star that seems to have strayed the most. When she interviewed David just a few years ago, he was enamored with her vision and seemed perfectly aligned with the mission of the firm. In fact, Diana recalls a company meeting last year when she asked for volunteers to retell the "True North" story instead of her. An eager David quickly stepped forward and articulated the value proposition perfectly. *What has changed? How had David drifted so far off course?*

Diana carefully contemplates her interactions with David and can't recall a single conversation where she heard anything "off-brand" that required intervention. Diana wonders if she was looking at David through rose-colored glasses. *Was she seeing what she wanted to see because her hopes for him were so high?*

> *Is there anyone you see through rose-colored glasses?*

Many of Diana's hopes for David were selfish in nature. David was enthusiastic and willing to do the work that nobody else wanted to do. Diana was just as eager to develop him as a protégé that could someday allow her to focus on public speaking and evangelism rather than day-to-day operations. Diana was tired and she was hoping David would be "the one" she could depend on to realize her dreams. At this point, Diana realizes that it is time to speak with David with a more impartial perspective.

In their conversation, Diana still finds David to be passionate about the company mission and driven to deliver results for their clients. He is particularly motivated by the new incentive program.

David further explains that the new program is appealing to him because it works on the same principles that drive their business with clients. The firm's clients pay for material reductions in carbon emissions and increases in energy efficiency– the numbers don't lie. In the same manner, the new incentive program shows how the contributions of individual employees lead to those same client outcomes that drive the business. David's only complaint is that he is so busy rolling out the whole program that he feels isolated from his peers and is frustrated by their lack of commitment to this groundbreaking initiative.

Diana recalls her recent client conversations and realizes that the focus on measurable outcomes is clouding other equally important objectives. Strong and productive relationships, mutual respect, leadership, and transparency are hallmarks of how the firm has built such a great reputation. *How could David have lost sight of this equally important intent?*

---

**_Does your organization have any objectives that compete with organizational values?_**

---

And then, like a ton of bricks, Diana understands what went wrong. She has done nothing but praise David for his work on the incentive program and the measurements he finds so compelling. While important, Diana has not given David any feedback on how he is measuring up to the "True North" principles that showcase respectful relationships. Diana just assumed that David knew how the two concepts complemented one another.

But before she celebrates her new revelation, Diana wonders why her long-time staff did not intervene and alert David to several flaws in the incentive program rollout. At the very least, they could have come to her and voiced their concerns. *Why were they silent?*

Naturally, this prompts Diana to speak with a few of her most loyal and trusted confidants. After a few glasses of wine and a wonderful dinner, a painful reality begins to emerge.

Initially, the "old guard" was comfortable with David stepping up to roll out the incentive plan. They were all very busy with work, and being at least ten years further into their careers, occupied with family and other community obligations. However, as the program rolled out, they felt that David was placing too much importance on the new program and not respecting the tried-and-true values that got the firm to this point in the first place. As a result, they began to resent how he overlooked the foundation they helped put in place. Any time David would harp on them for a lack of participation… they simply ignored him.

Diana wonders how she could have been so blind to the reputation David was building with her most loyal and devoted employees. This prompts her to ask one last biting question of her dearest colleagues: *"Why didn't you at least come to me when all of this was happening?"*

The answer reveals itself in a rather clumsy fashion. After several minutes of continuous and awkward praise, Diana learns that her colleagues thought so highly of her that they did not dare question the authority she had given to David. They felt that any criticism of the "anointed" David could be perceived as a criticism of Diana; something they were terribly uncomfortable doing to someone they admired so much. This adoring sentiment from her colleagues fills Diana with pride, but also heightens her awareness of how distanced she may have become from the realities within her organization.

Even though David has been disregarded by some of her most loyal employees, Diana knows he is a good person and that his heart is in the right place. Unfortunately, he was allowed to go for too long without any constructive or corrective feedback. And without

any productive feedback from Diana or her most experienced consultants, David was doomed to fail.

Diana realizes that feedback is not a "gift you receive," as the
saying goes. Feedback is something you need to actively seek and
provide. Without feedback, it is easy to stray off course and get out
of alignment.

Once again, Diana is strangely comforted by these uncomfortable realizations. One thing is for sure, she won't let her own pride
be her downfall.

# 7

# BEING TOO BUSY

Without a doubt, the most common business symptom is being too busy. From the executive ranks to the line worker, everyone is "crazy busy." As far as comparisons to medical symptoms, you would think that the pervasiveness of being busy makes it similar to the very common symptom of having a fever. This comparison, however, is not the best representation. Busyness is not like having a fever because you only get a fever when you are sick. People are too busy all the time. In fact, it might be more noticeable that you are not busy rather than too busy.

Being too busy is more like being dehydrated. You may not know this, but 75% of Americans are chronically dehydrated on a daily basis. What is astounding is that the negative effects of dehydration include decreases in cognition, mood, and mental agility. So, nearly three quarters of the population of one of the world's busiest countries could benefit by simply drinking a bit of water, but they elect not to. Puzzling...

In the same way that we unconsciously deal with the negative effects of dehydration, we do the same with our crazy busy lifestyles. We know we shouldn't be as busy as we are, yet we accept our frenetic lifestyles much as we deny ourselves the appropriate amount of water daily. Why then do we allow ourselves to persist in a state of constant busyness?

In order to understand this conundrum, it makes sense to start our examination at the *individual level*. Like many of life's great mysteries, though, it is often useful to look at the problem from a different perspective. Rather than look at why we fail to see the benefit of being less busy, it is more illustrative for us to examine why we chose —and possibly prefer— to live in a state of constant activity and stimulation.

After a fair amount of research on why we possibly prefer busyness, some consistent and interesting trends reveal themselves (Crabbe, 2014; Bellazza, Paharia, & Keinan, 2016).

The list of reasons has been whittled down to six and ordered from the more reasonable to the most irrational to understand:

- **Necessity**– Whether we feel pressure to keep our job or work multiple jobs, the desire to secure our future is a powerful motivator. Busyness is an outward display of productivity, commitment, and loyalty to any employer. If you need to keep a job, you work hard to look busy.

- **Status**– Many cultures view busyness as a badge of honor that raises an individual's social status. In countries where people are deemed to be socially mobile —that is, hard work pays off— being busy is a way to increase your social capital. Being busy means you are in demand and that demonstrates how you are valued in society. A busy restaurant is a good restaurant... right?

- **Ease**– Prioritizing what is important and what can wait is a difficult and never-ending chore. If we let our emails, meeting invites and text messages prioritize for us, we assume other people will be happy. Ironically, when we do this, we systematically give everyone else a vote in our priorities while denying ourselves a say in what should occupy our time. It takes courage to say no and potentially disappoint others. Choosing to be reactive to external requests for our time is an easy escape from difficult decisions and conversations.

- **FOMO**– Nobody likes being left out. This feeling is established in early childhood and exerts an influence well into adulthood. Information has always had value, but living in the "Information Age" means its currency has never been stronger. Hearing things first and being in-the-know are strong forces that make us attend more meetings and read more emails than are likely necessary.

- **Routine**– There are certain things we do that frequently serve no purpose or provide marginal benefit. We continue to do them, never questioning their value, because taking the time to figure it out would take more time out of our day. Our priorities may not be served by continuing these tasks, but today is simpler if we just keep doing what has always been done. Routine is what deceives us into prioritizing today over tomorrow.

- **Avoidance**– We all procrastinate. Frequently, when we procrastinate, we discover strange tasks that elevate in priority for mysterious reasons. Rooms are cleaned. Papers are filed. Projects are started. Regardless of what new tasks gain priority, we often create diversions to take our attention away from activities we loathe. Comically, we would be better off doing nothing when we procrastinate. Instead, we create new projects and task lists out of guilt- further exacerbating our hectic pace.

The truth is that the responsibility for this crazy-busy existence falls entirely on our own shoulders. We don't have to instantly read every new email. We don't have to attend every meeting we are invited to. We could make the time to focus on getting fewer more important things done. Instead, we consciously elect to be distracted by constant activity and stimulation. The decision to engage in non-essential work is what distinguishes *busyness* from a lack of *agency*.

When we examine busyness at the *interpersonal level*, it is once again important to look at the problem from a different perspective. The concept of leisure and "free-time" only became part of the average human condition in modern times. Throughout most of history, humans have worked in small groups to hunt for food and farm the land just to survive another day. Except for very wealthy upper classes, "free time" is a concept that is relatively new to the average person. In fact, a significant portion of the world's population still lives under the pressure to scratch out an existence each and every day.

The good news is that we are wired to work hard. Humans wouldn't have survived this long if working hard was not part of our DNA. Additionally, one of our best human traits is to work together to survive. Our strength as a species lies in our capacity to form tribes and our ability to collaborate. We are wired to help one another in the quest to survive.

Our affinity to collaborate is well documented by anthropologists and scientifically proven through countless psychology experiments. Some of the most fascinating research explores the deep-seated nature of our inclination to help others in need. One of the more interesting studies concluded that just adding the word "because" followed by *any* rationale to a request increases compliance by approximately 50% (Langer, 1978).

Understanding our compulsion to help others allows us to better comprehend why we let external requests drive our daily priority. If we view emails, meeting invitations, and chat messages as small requests for help, we can see how they trigger our internal drive to assist a friend in need.

But if requests for help are so powerful, why then does delegation in the workplace tend to be so difficult? We all know that delegation is one of the more important and critical skills for businesses to scale and distribute workloads. How is it that our human instincts to pitch in and help do not seem to be as strong when we are delegating?

Perhaps the most important reason why we are frequently disappointed with delegation is exactly because we mistake it to be a request or a transactional passing of responsibility. Worse yet, when delegating, we often *tell* people what to do rather than *ask* them for help. When we delegate in that manner, we immediately remove the unconscious compulsion to help a colleague and curtail the natural motivation that would otherwise work to our benefit.

Done properly, delegation is a collaborative process that requires engagement from both parties and takes place over a period of time. Delegation is not a simple request. Effective delegation is a skill that requires clarity of outcomes, adequate training, coaching and encouragement. Put simply, delegating properly takes a lot of time. And when we don't have time, we take shortcuts… and that is why delegation is usually a poorly developed skill that provides disappointing results. It is a vicious trap that further perpetuates a hesitancy to delegate and propagates continued busyness.

When we explore busyness at the *organizational level,* it is interesting to note that we have simultaneously mastered and over-complicated the concepts that influence how we cooperate in civilized society. Our earliest organizations were the tribes and cities that formed the building blocks of human civilization over 5000 years ago. That is when humans began to specialize the labor force to focus efforts on specific tasks. This ensured that everyone was fed, clothed, protected and sheltered. In time, daily survival became less of a burden, allowing for the development of interests like the arts, philosophy, and sports that were not directly related to basic human survival.

You would think that millennia later, organizations and businesses –the apex of modern civilization– would have mastered the art of focus and prioritization. Unfortunately, we're still not there. We have mastered some of these techniques, but we have also created new burdens that contribute to our frenzied existence. The three specific burdens we have created are *Resource Hoarding, Over-Optimization,* and *Infinite Priorities.*

What is fascinating is that these three burdens align well with the human motivations outlined in Daniel Pink's illuminating book, *Drive: The Surprising Truth About What Motivates Us.* His book identifies autonomy, mastery, and purpose as the key influencers of personal motivation.

*Resource Hoarding* aligns well with the human motivation of autonomy. Staffing levels have a significant impact on the autonomy of any work group in an organization. In modern business, we know that any allotment for additional headcount is a fleeting bounty that must be seized before the opportunity disappears. And since headcount losses rarely coincide with a decrease in the amount of work that is required, preserving headcount is a critical issue and a well-developed skill for seasoned corporate veterans. Headcount is a scarce resource in most organizations, and a key factor in group performance, individual happiness and how much power a leader appears to hold. In many ways, protecting scarce resources like headcount is a way to protect a leader's autonomy.

Leaders engage in countless schemes to ensure their people are busy and are seen as essential in furtherance of the business. Reduction in force discussions are passionate justifications of necessity and critical importance. Any outward appearance of being less busy damages the argument to retain headcount. As a result, visibly demonstrating high levels of activity can sometimes outweigh adequate levels of productivity allowing activity to be a surrogate for achievement: "Of course, we would like to accomplish more, but we're so darn busy!"

From the assembly line to modern computing, we have figured out how to squeeze incredible productivity out of each person and each minute in every day. However, the efficiencies we gain are rarely applied to personal growth, training, reflection, or strategic thinking. Every ounce of productivity is poured back into our enterprises to further improve performance. Unfortunately, we tend to optimize for ideal conditions. Put simply, we staff for steady-state conditions instead of peak workloads. Staffing for peak circumstances is counter-productive because we would look less busy *most* of the time. We are better off staffing for normal conditions and kicking into high gear for the occasional peak situation.

It would be easy to call this profiteering or greed, but it is much more than that. Profits equate to success and losses signify failure. We are obsessed with efficiency because nobody wants to be perceived as a failure. Optimization signals competence whereas inefficiency communicates incompetence. However self-defeating, *Over-Optimization* is a steroid-laced outward expression of mastery fueled by intense competition for position and power.

> "The word priority came into the English language in the 1400s. It was singular. It meant the very first or prior thing. It stayed singular for the next five hundred years. Only in the 1900s did we pluralize the term and start talking about priorities. Illogically, we reasoned that by changing the word we could bend reality."
> – Greg McKeown, *Essentialism: The Disciplined Pursuit of Less*

When I first read this passage, my mind was blown. I had not realized that the concept of multiple priorities was something new. In fact, the plural usage of the word priority only started to gain popularity in the 1940s when the industrialization of the modern world kicked into high gear for the war effort. Multiple fronts in the war of wars sensibly required multiple priorities. These exceptional circumstances had the entire world working with purpose to support their part of the war effort. But these were not just jobs that needed to get done, they were efforts with material purpose.

A hard day's work would help sailors with new boats, pilots with new planes and soldiers with more bullets. Every sheet of steel, aluminum rivet, or brass casing served a greater purpose than the simple mechanical task at hand. As Dan Pink suggests, having a purpose is a strong motivator.

Businesses learned the power of purpose and have wielded this motivational tool in ways that are both admirable and questionable. Whether we were supporting shareholder value, customer delight, or a better world, assigning meaning to our work makes a difference. And the greater the meaning, the more important the work– right? And by extension, what if we were to have bigger purposes –or even– multiple purposes? Our work would even be more important– right?

And that is exactly what we have done. We have created mission statements, stretch goals, and management objectives to handle our complex purpose-driven agendas. We support those efforts with project plans, collaboration tools and complex spreadsheets that coordinate and align our efforts. That does not mean that our intentions aren't pure. In most cases, they are. However, our intentions often fail to be complete.

Our stretch goals can often stretch us too far. Our insatiable appetite for new projects often ignores the need for meetings where we say "no" to new initiatives. Our status reports wouldn't be thick enough and our meetings wouldn't be long enough to justify our budgets, headcounts, and importance. How can any amount of work be validated if the underlying goal is not sufficiently worthy? How can we be satisfied with a modest singular goal that could be expressed simply? How can we justify our staffing levels, or the next hire, if we aren't pressing against the limits of our capacity?

This is the world we have created. This is the world we live in. This is a reality that is based on activity over achievement. This is the world where we are all too busy.

■ ■ ■

Diana's identity is tied closely to the business she started ten years ago. Owning a business consumes you in ways that are hard to describe. There is no "nine-to-five" when you are an entrepreneur. There is nobody to take your place when you are on vacation. It is exhausting, but being busy is a fact of life that Diana has begrudgingly accepted.

In the past several weeks, Diana has gathered a tremendous amount of insight about the current state of her firm. The more she reviews the situation the deeper her understanding becomes. She is now painfully aware of how deeply overworked her team has become.

> ### *Are you, or anyone working for you, overworked?*

The team Diana originally recruited has been with her for many years and knows the grind. They are used to the long hours and hard work required to support environmental changes for their clients. The work is purposeful and rewarding, but it can be stressful and hectic.

Not sure of what exactly has changed, Diana reviews some of the facts:

- The company has been growing rapidly and so has the workload on consultants.
- Clients have remarked that many of Diana's consultants seem tired and stressed.

- Turnover has kept the benefit of new hires in check.
- Training requirements for new employees further decreases availability for client work.
- The new incentive program that has been led by David has not been received well. It was supposed to balance workloads, but few managers have found the time to implement the new methods.
- The benefit of the incentive program is only realized after it is broadly adopted by the entire organization.
- David has made several missteps by telling the managers what to do instead of asking for their help.
- A level of resentment has developed and the camaraderie that has been typical of the organization seems to have faded.

Diana has come to expect a sense of peace and relief after thoughtful reflections such as this. There is no peace today. Diana's heart is racing, and she fears she may have lost control of the situation. Her successful growing company feels like it is on the verge of crumbling. As she fights back tears, she wonders how she was too busy to notice all these changes.

Sensing her deep level of dismay, Diana's husband Dean suggests they go out to dinner that evening. Perhaps some good comfort food and a glass of wine will make everything better. For the first 30 minutes, all Diana can do is lament her situation. After a while they order their food, drink some wine and sit in relative silence until their meals arrive.

When the meals arrive, they are on oversized plates with heaping portions of traditional ethnic dishes that normally delight Diana. Solidly in a funk, though, all Diana can think about is how much food is going to go to waste. She makes a snarky comment about the massive portions to Dean and expects him to agree with her. He does not.

Dean quickly responds with a different perspective. He reminds Diana of what it was like when they were young, he was in med school, and she was working two jobs to support them. They didn't have much money or time together. Meals were cheap and often eaten in a hurry as their busy schedules only offered a precious few minutes together each evening. In an understanding yet decidedly firm voice, he lets Diana know how lucky they are to have this much food to eat. They can enjoy fine wine, delicious cuisine and still have leftovers for lunch tomorrow. There is no need to eat everything in one sitting. There is no need to complain.

Later that evening, Diana realizes that she is blessed. Her business has plenty of "food" on its plate. They don't have to eat it all.

The next day, Diana convenes her managers for an emergency meeting. She outlines the crisis as she sees it and makes some stark confessions to the team:

- Diana acknowledges that everyone is busy with work and life. The pace they are working at is not healthy for them or the business.
- Diana concedes that she poorly delegated the incentive program to David without properly preparing him or the rest of the team.
- Diana also acknowledges that allowing David to demand compliance was an ineffective strategy she should have stopped.
- Diana humbles herself and apologizes for undermining the autonomy of her team and devaluing their expertise (mastery).

The sense of relief within Diana's management team is palpable. They too thought the company was in peril. With the seal broken, they also share some confessions:

- Nobody wanted or felt they could handle the extra work.
- The managers protected their team to make sure their projects didn't suffer.
- Even when consultants had some extra time, they kept that quiet for fear of losing them to another project or David's incentive program rollout.
- They felt comfortable with their social standing and didn't feel obligated to take on more to prove their worth.
- They are used to the way they have always done things. They did not realize that the benefit of the incentive program is only realized after a majority of the team adopts the system.
- Admittedly, they just didn't know what the top priority was. Client success? The incentive program? Growth? The "True North" principles?

While nothing has been resolved, a sense of relief and calm has put this crisis in perspective. It appears her team wants to weather this storm with her. The key will be to decide what NOT to do.

> ***What could you decide not to do?***

# 8

## CONFLICT

We can dream of a world without conflict, but it is entirely unrealistic. Conflict is, and always will be, part of the human condition. The absence of conflict is neither peace nor harmony. The absence of conflict is apathy. This is why conflict should not be avoided, but rather why it should be understood and embraced. Conflict is a necessary part of how any idea gets sharper, any product gets better, and any business gets stronger.

While conflict is undesirable and messy, it is quite simple to understand. It has three fundamental components. At least two people, with at least two opinions and a reluctance to compromise. If any of these three components are missing, you do not have conflict, but rather, a discussion or a negotiation. It is the nature of the final element, the reluctance to compromise, that defines whether conflict is a destructive or productive process.

People decide to dig their heels in and stand firm for a variety of reasons. At the simplest level, people stand firm because of a conviction to an ideal or a passion for a cause. In other cases, people can be uninformed, ignorant, or unwilling to accept information that would soften a hardline position. However, embedded in all conflict is a lack of trust, empathy, or respect for the counterparty in a relationship.

To think conflict is about winning arguments is to think you can win at relationships. Nobody wins relationships and relationships don't improve without empathy, respect, and trust. The anticipation of conflict, or the avoidance thereof, is a tacit acknowledgement of a relationship that could be stronger. It is how we choose to handle conflict that determines whether relationships heal or fracture.

The key to successfully using conflict to sharpen an idea, improve an outcome, or build a stronger relationship is to understand that conflict takes many forms. The two basic types of intragroup conflict are task and relationship conflict (Jehn, 1995). Task conflict focuses on the outcome of a task and allows teams to critique results to improve performance. In fact, the highest performing teams and the military successfully maintain a focus on task conflict to improve overall team performance (Walker, 2017). Keeping the focus on processes and common goals allow task conflict to be the safest and most benign of the two because the area of concern is kept at the organizational level.

When the dialogue devolves into personal attacks, we have descended to relationship conflict. Once this happens, interpersonal issues between team members elevate into emotional judgments and heated disputes over personal differences. Relationship conflict almost always degrades team performance.

Unfortunately, the skill to navigate conflict and shepherd the process away from relationship conflict toward more productive and positive outcomes is a rare talent; even when the necessary blueprint for navigating such conflict is outlined clearly in books like *The Disconnect Principle* by Ann Latham. Those rare individuals that develop this skill and have the courage to apply it in their business dealings typically achieve success that others envy.

What makes conflict so fascinating is that it is often seen as the root cause of a problem rather than a symptom. Both conflict and the avoidance of conflict are not problems, they are the penultimate symptoms of actual problems. And those problems always have to do with a relationship that could be in better shape. Troubled relationships may not be the ultimate business problem we need to address, but they are the embers that can fuel any problem into a full-blown crisis.

There are entire branches of psychology that are written on the internal conflict one may have within their own psyche. We will not cover that. What we will cover is the interpersonal conflict that happens within teams and the conflict that happens between groups in any organization.

At the *interpersonal level*, conflict is a marker for an underlying business problem the same way pain in your left arm is a warning sign for a heart attack. Like a serious heart condition, conflict is an acute symptom of a serious problem and needs to be addressed with urgency and caution. As obvious as this may be, many people with undiagnosed heart conditions frequently ignore warning signs for months and years while their condition worsens. Similarly, people avoid conflict even though the warning signs exist long before any crisis emerges.

We avoid difficult conversations with employees. We dread tough discussions with vendors. We delay awkward conversations with clients. All these situations are common in business and typical of relationships that could be stronger. Much like a healthy diet and exercise would stave off many heart issues, maintaining rich and respectful relationships would prevent most conflict. And while we know it is in our best interest to prevent or address conflict, there are powerful incentives to push it off for another day.

Foremost of these incentives is time. Developing and maintaining good relationships is very time consuming. Similarly, the time and effort required to change dietary routines and develop new exercise habits is an intimidating barrier that often delays any meaningful efforts to improve one's health. The cruel irony is that investing in an improved diet and cardio routine is no guarantee that you will avoid heart issues. The same is true for relationships. You can invest in relationships and still end up in conflict.

Additionally, addressing and diffusing conflict is a risky proposition. In business, part of what makes conflict resolution so risky is that you really can't win but you can always lose. A successful outcome is an improved and more functional relationship– something that is expected to have been there in the first place. Furthermore, the process of adjudicating and resolving any conflict often reveals hard truths and stark realizations that can be overly transparent and embarrassing for everyone involved. As such, many business problems are exacerbated purely because we emotionally fear being exposed and logically avoid situations with limited upside and larger downside risks.

The problem with avoiding conflict is twofold. First, if there is a problem brewing, it is always better to address it sooner rather than later. General Colin Powell famously said, *"Bad news isn't wine. It doesn't improve with age."* The second and more profound issue is that perceived conflict is often imagined conflict. Put simply, sometimes there just isn't any conflict of significance. As stated earlier, our imaginations never take us to a rational outcome. And once our imaginations and fears engage, the downside risk of conflict can inflate to levels far beyond reason. These two forces, working in concert, can sow the seeds for greater conflict.

When we do work up the nerve to address a situation we fear may result in conflict, we often back down and fail to be direct enough with our communication. We can't resist the temptation to soften the sharp edges of potential conflict and candy coat messages that could be perceived as negative. In our efforts to masterfully pilot our discussion through turbulent waters we often steer ourselves, and the relationship, aground. Any time we water down the discussion, ignoring the "elephant in the room", we compromise authenticity and raise suspicions. In these cases, we frequently increase the same tensions and fears that tempted us to back off from the position we knew we should have taken in the first place. Preempting conflict and conducting difficult discussions is not easy.

At the *organizational level*, outright conflict is less common than you might think. While individual tempers may flare and arguments may take place, it is rare to have an entire workgroup postured aggressively against another group. However, when workgroups lack trust, empathy, or respect for one another, conflict can emerge.

The reason all-out conflict within an organization is rare is because everyone, to some degree, must live together under the same roof. Additionally, from a leadership perspective, there is very little incentive to allow conflict between groups to overshadow company goals. It is a far smarter political move to let any serious conflict appear as a disagreement between individuals within those groups.

Some degree of political conflict is inevitable in all organizations. Whether it is jockeying for scarce resources (people, budget, bonuses, etc.) or plain old competition between groups, it is a guarantee that humans will be human and someone will say or do something hurtful. The key is whether the groups can come together, compromise, and collaborate effectively when needed.

The situation becomes problematic when the trends and frequency of individual instances of conflict structurally adhere to patterns across many members of a particular group. Marketing never gets their forecasts to us on time. Shipping drags their feet all day so they can work overtime. Finance never invites us to Taco Tuesday. Whatever the reason, conflict becomes an organizational issue when patterns and trends of behavior start to breed resentment between internal tribes. Although many of these "departmental" rivalries and rifts can seem as though they are shared by the entire group, most instances merely reflect ongoing interpersonal conflict between the leaders of those groups. Humans have a strange way of adopting the views and personality of their leaders as their own. In these cases, the negative impact is usually limited to productivity and workplace harmony.

For conflict to truly exist at the organizational level, it must be structural. In these circumstances, conflict will present itself in the form of understood political rivalries and tensions that breed contempt and bad feelings. If you couple that with some tribal identity and a refusal to compromise, you have a recipe for organizational conflict. Manufacturing doesn't like Sales. The Houston office doesn't like the Denver office. The Food and Beverage Division doesn't like the Housewares Division. You get the drift.

The good news about internal company conflict is that it rarely gets to the level of existential survival. Unless a branch office is getting closed or a division is being shut down, people will still have to work together. This reason alone is why internal company conflict tends to be self-limiting in intensity.

Externally, conflict tends to happen under very specific circumstances. It is only when one party feels or is beholden to another party that the conditions for conflict are set. Otherwise, parties that are not deeply connected can decide to part and go their own ways. Put simply, it's easy to take your business elsewhere.

The situation changes when you can't take your business elsewhere. Whether there is deep technology integration, proprietary methods, or supply chain dependencies, things can get ugly and tempers can flare. The lack of alternatives can be a strong temptation for one side to feel there is no need to compromise. Similarly, the lack of recourse can provide a strong foundation for a desperate and uncompromising stance.

Add in money concerns (Large past-due balances, slow payment terms, contested invoices, etc.) and the situation becomes explosive. The rationale is that money establishes the method to measure if someone has "won" a business relationship. It is impossible to win at interpersonal relationships, but once we add in money, we have a construct to measure the success of any negotiation. And while most negotiations are not full-blown conflicts, many businesspeople are so unskilled at negotiation that they feel it is appropriate to take hardline positions that show little respect for their business partner.

Once again, any kind of conflict is still a symptom of a larger set of issues.

■ ■ ■

Everyone that works with Diana knows the one name that can send her into an emotional tirade. It's the name of her former partner... Donna!

Diana did not start in business alone. In the beginning, it was Diana and Donna. A power-duo of driven young executives with big ideas and even bigger dreams. The two became friends in graduate school and quickly formed a bond with one another. They collaborated on projects and shared similar visions for environmental best-practices that businesses could profitably implement. At the time, most people thought that profit and environmentalism were mutually exclusive goals. The tandem of Diana and Donna knew better.

The early years were fun, but they didn't last. In time, the alignment between the two faded and the distance between the pair grew. Their alignment on the mission and vision of the organization was never the source of their fracture, it had more to do with style. Diana and Donna's leadership styles were very different.

Diana is an inclusive and supportive leader. She does not see others as threats to her authority and therefore empowers everyone to learn and grow with her. Donna saw things differently. Donna's style was controlling and authoritative. Her skills were useful when they were managing a project with tight budgets and deadlines, but they were caustic for growing a team and a company. As time passed, Diana was seen as the visionary leader of the organization while Donna was viewed much less favorably by the staff and clients. Donna had a role to play in the organization, but it was not the leadership role she wanted… or thought she deserved as a co-founder.

---

### *Have you experienced any stylistic clashes?*

---

The result was a split. A business divorce. These can be painful and costly affairs. This case was no different. With sufficient confidence in herself and the comfort Dean's successful career afforded, Diana chose to exit the company with terms that favored Donna greatly but allowed her the freedom to end the process quickly and start again on her own. Many saw this as a loss for Diana and victory for Donna. Diana knew better.

Ten years later, Diana has a successful business that is well-respected in the community. Diana's business has grown steadily, while Donna's business is no bigger than the day Diana left. And while Donna's business has stumbled along working one project at a time, she maintains a small and highly competent staff. Even though these facts could give Diana great comfort in her decision, she is still raw from the concessions she made and the indignation she endured.

However, Diana does realize that Donna held her back. She also acknowledges that she never would have established the guiding principles of her "True North" story if it were not for the stark contrast between her and Donna's leadership style. Even with all these affirmations, thinking about those days still hurts.

> *Can you think of a bad situation that eventually turned into a blessing?*

With more "food on her plate" than her company can eat, Diana knows she needs to start making some different decisions. She either needs to turn away some business, delay some engagements, or seek outside help to keep her team from being overwhelmed.

Diana considers engaging Donna to help with her backlog of work. Donna's project management expertise could be a huge help on her biggest and most complex project. After much pondering, Diana decides that would be a bad idea. Donna's uncompromising style might bring a level of toxicity and conflict into an important client relationship.

Instead, Diana opts to keep her distance from Donna and the stress that goes with all the baggage from their divorce. Her plan is to contact three of the clients that are looking to start new projects with her in the coming weeks and discuss alternatives. One option would be to refer those clients to Donna's firm. And while the mere thought of "giving" projects to Donna noticeably raises Diana's stress level, having her firm implode under the pressure of too much work is an outcome that would be more crushing.

Diana knows that this approach would provide time to retrench with her team and oversee the changes that would allow them to address the turnover crisis and work more efficiently. It is the right decision, but a bitter pill to swallow. Diana agonizes over this decision and dreads the phone calls she knows are necessary.

That evening Diana plays out the phone calls in her head. Her imagination is running wild, and her thoughts are filled with worst-case scenarios:

- What will she say to Donna?
- How will her clients react?
- Will this hurt the reputation of the firm she has poured her heart and soul into?
- Will Donna poison important client relationships she has been fostering for years?
- Will Donna be smug about this and make it feel like yet another defeat?

The morning arrives and all the calls are made. After it is all said and done, it is not as painful as Diana had imagined it would be. Two of her three clients agree to delay their projects for a full quarter. One client is very understanding and respects the value of Diana and her firm. They are willing to wait for the "best-in-class" service Diana's firm has a reputation for delivering. Much to her surprise, a second client was already planning on calling her about delaying the start of their engagement as they were behind schedule with some of their internal planning.

The third client is interested in an introduction to Donna and her firm. They are on a tight timeline for their capital project and delays would be very costly. Diana's explanation of being too busy was frustrating to them, but they were not as upset as she would have predicted. They were disappointed about a misleading sales experience, but they were very appreciative of the up-front acknowledgment of limitations that could threaten their project timeline.

The dreaded conversation with Donna was not as bad as expected. Although Donna was indeed a bit smug at times, it was clear she could use the business. Before Donna could ask, Diana made it clear that she was not looking for a finder's fee or commission for this referral. There were no strings attached. No conflict. No Drama.

# 9

## CULTURE

Culture is the ultimate business symptom. The reasoning for this is that culture is an incredibly broad co-indicator of other problems and symptoms plaguing a business. People often refer to company cultures as being either good or bad. Perhaps we should view cultures differently– sick and healthy.

A company culture is, in many ways, exactly like the immune system of a human being. Sick cultures are vulnerable to small external influences in the same way unhealthy people are more susceptible to viruses and infection.

When market externalities arrive in the form of declining economic conditions, pricing pressure or competition, unhealthy cultures do not fend off these "viruses" as gracefully as a healthy company. Under stress, unhealthy cultures also produce additional side effects like conflict and misalignment to name a few. Unhealthy cultures tend to get sicker when stressed.

Healthy cultures, however, are like a human being with a strong immune response. Strong cultures have less conflict, more alignment, and more predictable expectations. In the same way that healthy people can run at peak operating tempo, organizations with healthy cultures can handle busier schedules and produce more results.

But immune systems and organizational cultures share a similar trait-- you can't easily replace them. In the grand scheme of things, you can only do things to influence your immune system to perform better. You can eat healthier, you can exercise, and you can supplement your diet with vitamins, but there is no way to directly alter your immune response. Even a vaccine, perhaps the most direct method of boosting your immune response, is still acting as an influence on a system you can't directly change. Just like your immune system, the culture of an organization is something you can only influence.

Compare culture to your personal reputation. You may be able to influence your reputation, but you do not own it. Your customers, your partners, and the market define your reputation. They are in charge. Culture is similar.

Culture is a manifestation of an organization's values. And while you can declare and define your values, culture doesn't abide by them. Culture has a mind of its own. The firm hand on the wheel that sets forth a company's culture is evident in everyday decisions. Where is capital invested? How is time devoted? Where are resources allocated? All of these are questions that beg decisions that further inform what an organization deems most important. The values that survive the inevitable conflicts associated with scarce resources are the truest measure of what a company treasures most. It is these triumphant values that define the culture of a company.

Many organizations have a somewhat schizophrenic culture or no culture at all. Their decisions are inconsistent and even contradictory in some cases. This sets the conditions for a weak or non-existent culture. Many of these companies are described with eloquent words and firm devotions, but nobody truly believes them.

Organizations with strong cultures possess an inherent consistency in their decision making. There is a pattern that governs daily decision making from the very top of the organization down to the lowest levels. Whether quality is job #1 or maximizing share-holder value is the guiding principle, consistency in decision making is what creates a strong culture.

Some would argue that a good culture serves a virtuous purpose, whereas a bad culture is misaligned with a more unethical or unacceptable intent. This is a misleading way to evaluate organizational culture. Good or bad describes a value judgment on the culture, rather than the health or strength of that culture. It is always important to note that one person's "good" culture can be another person's prison. Judging the correctness of organizational culture is as foolish as dismissing musical genres based on taste. Consensus is a foolhardy pursuit.

Perhaps the ideal way to look at culture is to evaluate whether it is weak or strong. Weak cultures are inconsistent, difficult to predict, and therefore hard to trust. Strong cultures are the epitome of consistency, confidence, and trust. And the very strongest of cultures are forged when decisions are difficult, and the stakes are high.

Will quality remain at the forefront of the decision-making process when quarterly profits may disappoint?

Culture is the ultimate reflection of an organization's values which are determined by the decisions that are made on a daily basis.

■ ■ ■

As an entrepreneur, Diana has always viewed the culture of her organization as a reflection of her own integrity and values. Diana's involvement in nearly every aspect of the business ensured that her "touch" was present in all that they did. The consistency in how they conducted business was not only a great source of pride for Diana, but it was also a tremendous foundation of confidence for the team and all their clients. In many ways, the strong company culture has been the backbone of their success.

But it was becoming clear to Diana that the culture she worked hard to establish was not the culture she has today. What was once a source of tremendous strength is starting to feel like more of a liability. This is a disturbing thought for Diana, that poses many questions:

- What had happened?
- Has the culture truly changed?
- The "True North" story has not changed... What did?
- How has her team gotten so far off track?
- Has she changed?

These are tough questions with no simple answers. As she thinks about these questions, feelings of self-doubt begin to enter her mind and sap her confidence.

> ### *Who do you speak with when your confidence is low?*

Diana's husband Dean, her most trusted confidant, has been with her through this entire journey. Building the company has been a shared experience for both of them —the highs as well as the lows. When she turns to Dean for advice, he always starts by asking questions, just like any good physician would do. Through this deliberative process, they arrive at several conclusions:

- Diana has not changed and neither has the "True North" foundation she communicates to her team.
- The new incentive program, which is intended to help the company grow and scale, is likely emphasizing decision making that is in conflict with the original vision and culture of her firm.

- It appears a cultural divide exists between the newer consultants and the "old guard" who has been with Diana since the early days.
- The "old guard" is held in high regard by everyone.
- Newer employees, such as David, are eager to gain the respect of the "old guard."
- The "old guard" enjoys their position of respect and is not welcoming to new employees.
- David's aggressive approach to demand compliance –in the name of Diana for the new incentive program– was not received well by the "old guard."
- David is the only male manager in her firm. This makes acceptance by the all-female "old guard" even more challenging.
- New ways of thinking about the business and the growth plans are not universally accepted, shared, or understood.

Diana scratches her head after her discussion with Dean. Nothing they spoke about was a revelation to her. She was aware of everything that was going on. The only mistake Diana made was that she thought the culture was strong enough to correct and align her team. The culture was the backbone of her business and she believed it would keep everyone aligned.

For years, Diana had thought that company culture was the foundation of her business. Stable. Firm. Dependable. But culture is nothing like the foundation of a building. What Diana now realizes is that culture is a dynamic state that must be closely managed and maintained. In many ways, culture is more like the landscaping outside her building. Culture requires constant maintenance and attention. Pruning of weeds, fertilization of flowers, and mowing of grass is a never-ending responsibility. And when culture is left alone, it does not take long for the weeds to spring up and suffocate the flowers.

What confounds Diana is what she needs to do next. She could call an all-company meeting and talk about this, but she knows that won't solve anything. She could talk to David and the "old guard" and tell them to get along better. Once again, she knows the benefit will be temporary. What is it that will help repair and strengthen her beloved culture?

The answer does not arrive quickly. After a long week and many restless nights, Diana heads into the weekend without answers and without hope.

Instead of her usual podcast fueled Saturday morning run, Diana opts for a quiet solo walk in the woods. The change of scenery and the solitude allow her mind to relax and wander.

As she enters a clearing in the forest, she notices a hawk soaring above, carefully surveying the prairie grass. She watches as the hawk manages to observe the entire field as it circles overhead. The complexity of that undertaking is something Diana finds incredible. How do you watch an entire field? As she contemplates the problem, she considers that the predator may only be looking for movement against an unchanging backdrop. That is the only sensible way in which the hawk could process all this information. This thought inspires her. It is the small changes in her business she has failed to notice.

While powerful, her culture is not a singular guiding principle that governs the team. It is exactly the opposite. Her culture is the product of many small decisions and choices that happen daily. Culture is a pattern of behavior that is ever-changing. And if Diana does not start noticing inconsistencies with the patterns that support the culture she desires, the health of the company she loves will decline.

> *Do your daily decisions support your desired culture?*

# 10

## FOR GOOD MEASURE

As we begin to discuss the final three of the ten most common business symptoms, it is important to highlight a commonality they share. Each of the remaining symptoms, turnover, profitability, and growth can be measured.

While we could come up with creative ways to measure some of the earlier symptoms like accountability and conflict, there are no universal and undisputed methods to measure those symptoms. Any time there is a metric with room for interpretation, it is a guarantee that you are also untangling the complex narratives and justifications for both the measurement as well as the result.

For the final three symptoms, however, there are accepted and standardized ways in which results are measured. But just because something can be measured does not mean that it is the problem. Many things that can be measured remain symptoms of more deeply rooted core problems.

Perhaps the most common health metric we can measure is our weight. We know that being overweight increases the likelihood of diabetes, heart disease, and many other serious health problems. Being overweight is not good, but there is no guarantee that being trim prevents you from having a heart attack or diabetes either.

Additionally, there are plenty of people who are overweight who are healthy and even manage to run marathons. Being overweight is not the health problem. The health problem is diabetes or heart disease. Being overweight is just a risk factor that increases the odds of initiating the onset of a disease.

Good discipline with numbers and data is much like the good discipline of keeping your weight in check. It will not guarantee that you will avoid problems, but it can certainly increase the odds of a positive outcome.

# 11

# TURNOVER/RETENTION

Organizations do not benefit from the loss of expertise and efficiency that experienced and trained employees possess. The costs of recruiting and re-training new talent are not insignificant. Additionally, the burden of properly onboarding and integrating new talent is often underestimated. But even with a profound incentive to retain talent, organizations fail to address the core issues that drive employees away.

Perhaps the most puzzling aspect of turnover and retention is our impulsive first response to connect the issue to money. Countless articles, books, and research studies have proven that money is far down on the list of reasons why people leave organizations. Fair compensation is important but should be considered the "table stakes" for employment rather than the differentiator that drives employee satisfaction. The Gallup organization has done exceptional research in this area and has concluded that employees are far more likely to perceive that they are paid appropriately when they feel engaged at work (Gallup Employee Engagement Survey, 1990s–today). And if their co-workers are similarly engaged and committed, compensation issues generally take a back seat.

But money is a hasty target when turnover becomes problematic. Money is an easy explanation and a simple excuse. More money doesn't fix problems, it masks them. Money can hide or delay problems, but it does not address the core issue driving retention. Ask any Human Resources professional about the utility of counter-offers and you will learn that the benefit of more money is often short-lived.

The second most popular scapegoat in the world of employee retention is the "market." Hot job markets and competitive pressures are common themes when discussing turnover issues within companies. It is nice to think that our problems are not of our own making and certainly beyond our control. But happy employees do not seek solutions for problems that don't exist… even in hot job markets.

Market shifts merely accelerate events that were already in motion. A bad boss may be tolerable when the fears of unemployment are high. But as soon as gainful employment options become more promising, tolerating that bad boss seems wholly unreasonable. The changing job market is not the cause for an employee's departure, it is merely the tipping point on the scale. This same balancing act can apply to any number of other reasons why employees feel unsatisfied with their employer.

The Gallup organization has completed several groundbreaking studies that support the common business proverb that *"people leave managers, not companies."* In their comprehensive 2015 study on "The State of the American Manager," Gallup concluded that 50% of employees left a job in their career to get away from their manager. They also found that *"the manager accounts for at least 70% of the variance in employee engagement."*

These findings draw a sharp focus on a manager's impact on the factors that drive turnover and retention within organizations. The concept of a bad boss makes perfect sense, but it also feeds a deceptive and false narrative.

When we hear the term –a **bad boss**– our minds quickly go to a red-faced jerk yelling and screaming at their team. It is easy to paint the picture of a bad boss as an uncaring boor that insults and berates their employees. The problem with this imagery is that it misleads us into correlating a bad boss with being a bad person. A good person can also be a bad boss. The characteristics of a bad boss are different from the characteristics of a bad person. Perfectly wonderful people can be woefully poor at advocating for their team, managing workloads, failing to obtain the proper resources, and tolerating underperformance. People leave bosses when the boss is not good at their job.

As such, it is important to highlight the most notable frustrations employees have with their bosses:

- **Autonomy**– People have an innate desire to approach problems and work in a manner that suits their personal preferences. Everyone has an unspoken and sometimes subconscious comprehension of their own capabilities. As such, there is a strong preference to go about our business in the manner that suits our individual strengths and skill sets. When we are allowed to do this, we are operating with autonomy. When the freedom to use personal discretion is limited, employees often seek that freedom elsewhere. Good bosses don't micromanage and allow ample room for employees to exercise a prudent level of autonomy.

- **Lack of Growth or Personal Development**– It is in our human nature to seek mastery of our chosen professions. It is when that progression is stifled or arrested that employees take notice. Regardless of the pace or the intensity with which an individual may pursue their personal development, everyone prefers to have a path forward. Employees will explore other options when they feel the pace of their personal development is restricted by someone other than themselves. Good bosses facilitate employee growth and development.

- **Engagement or Lack of Connection**– People naturally desire connection and belonging. The fabric of our lives is driven by an innate need to be accepted as members of a family or tribe. Good mental health relies upon connection to others and a purpose for our existence. Work is no different. It is important for employees to feel connected with their co-workers, their boss, and a greater purpose. All three of these connections are important to employee satisfaction. Weakness in any of these areas can stir the motivation for an employee to explore new career options. Good bosses carefully monitor and cultivate these connections with their employees.

- **Workload and Resources**– All aspects of life contain varying levels of stress that ebb and flow with our circumstances. The stress we experience at work is an enormous factor influencing our happiness and our overall health. And while humans can tolerate impressive levels of stress, it is ineffective and unhealthy to operate at peak levels for prolonged periods of time. Managers who are unsuccessful at setting priorities, marshaling resources, and removing roadblocks increase the stress levels within their team. Chronically understaffed and under-resourced organizations eventually face significant retention issues. Good bosses adjust workloads and campaign for resources so employees can operate within reasonable levels of stress.

- **Recognition**– The need to be recognized is not about salary increases, bonuses, or even awards. Those are nice, but true recognition is about the very human need to be seen and appreciated. A simple thank you or a sincere statement of gratitude is often all that is needed. Even more important is peer recognition that boosts social standing and self-esteem.

In the absence of recognition, employees will find it elsewhere. Good bosses ensure their employees receive proper recognition.

- **Tolerating Poor Performers**– If you want to have top talent exit your organization, tolerate poor performance. Nothing gets superstars to leave your organization faster than saddling them with teammates that restrict their performance. Tolerating poor performance is an explicit signal that accountability is not universal and that rules and/or standards do not apply equally. Good bosses do not tolerate poor performance.

- **Poor Fit**– Issues of turnover are not always related to problems with retention. In some cases, hiring practices are to blame. This aspect of retention is often overlooked because it places blame squarely on the hiring authority rather than the employee. Turnover can be a direct result of hiring to the wrong profile. No amount of autonomy, good management or recognition will satisfy a person who does not fit their role or the organization. Good bosses make good hires.

Now this does not mean that every employee departure is a failure of management. In individual cases, employees may leave because they feel they are undeserving of criticism and worthy of merit. Having managed people for decades, I have hired people that were clearly deserving of criticism who expected unearned merit. Not all employee departures are heart wrenching experiences and setbacks.

However, broad retention issues typically signal a systemic concern that should alert any management team to take an introspective look at their practices and outcomes. This is why measurement is important. Measurement can help determine if retention issues are broad trends or isolated incidents.

It is also important to note that numeric figures are rarely as simple as they seem. A bad boss with an increasing rate of turnover may be revealed because market conditions are finally allowing employees to exercise the freedom to change. However, it is possible for that same bad boss to display a decreasing rate of turnover because poor market conditions are forcing employees to hunker down until the job market improves. In both cases the quality of the manager has not changed, but the numeric measurements can signal vastly different interpretations.

On any given day, priority should be given to good management practices. However, the reality of busy work schedules and competing urgencies often keep managers from being the best version of themselves. That is why it is important to notice when we stray away from the ideal behaviors of a good boss. Like the hawk circling above, close monitoring of turnover and retention trends can alert savvy management teams to take a reflective pause and correct course.

■ ■ ■

The pain of employee turnover has been crippling Diana's business for the last several months. Her business has been booming which means her services are also in high demand. Logically, demand is also very high for consultants who can guide companies through the intricacies of environmental impacts and regulations.

However, it is a surprise that *her* consultants are leaving. Diana thought that the passion, the integrity, and the culture of her firm would create an environment employees would never want to leave. On top of that, departing employees know what a difficult position this creates for Diana and the friends they leave behind. What had she missed?

Realizing that the market is hot for the talent she has on her team, Diana reaches out to her outsourced HR partner to find out what is going on in the marketplace. Perhaps there is a trend that had escaped her attention as she was busy growing her business.

While she waits for the HR firm to respond, Diana probes her management team to better understand the situation. All she gets in return is a chorus of complaints about compensation being the main reason for the recent surge in resignations. Diana asks her team if they know where people are going or how much more they are getting at their new companies. The response is not comforting.

Most of her team does not know these answers and it appears as though they didn't even ask any of the important questions that would allow them to halt the outpouring of talent. Diana wonders what questions are even being asked in the exit interviews they insist they are doing.

*Do you ever audit people and processes to ensure they are conforming to standards you worked hard to put in place?*

The deeper Diana digs into this situation the more exasperated she becomes. She feels the onset of a migraine and her patience is running thin with everyone. Diana makes the executive decision to conduct her own exit interview with an employee that recently resigned but was still working through a two-week transition phase. She calls her assistant and makes a point to meet this employee over breakfast.

The breakfast is with a sharp young consultant named Debbie. This was Debbie's first job out of college, but you would never know it by speaking with her. Debbie has tremendous potential and is adored by her clients.

Like a true professional, Diana starts the discussion with gratitude for Debbie's service and plenty of compliments for her work and her promising future. Debbie is not just appreciative, she is awestruck. Debbie confides to Diana that she is her hero. Ever since she heard Diana speak at an event while she was in college, Diana was someone she wanted to emulate. The opportunity to work with Diana was her *dream* job.

Confused, Diana asks an important question: *"So why would you leave your dream job?"*

Just pondering the question causes tears to well up in Debbie's eyes. Diana can tell she is going to get to the heart of the matter. Debbie's speech is slow and deliberate. She qualifies her statements with the following comment: *"I don't want to get anyone in trouble, so please do not share this."*

Debbie then proceeds to talk about her relationship with her supervisor. At first, she was honored to be working for such an esteemed member of the management team. She was excited to be mentored by someone that would help her follow in Diana's footsteps. But the way it turned out was not what she had expected. Her manager barely had time for her. In fact, 50 percent of her one-on-one meetings were habitually canceled at the last minute. Debbie did not feel valued and felt more like a resource than a human.

At this point tears are now starting to well up in Diana's eyes. How could this promising young woman get so jaded so fast? Where did they do wrong?

Diana then asks Debbie, *"Why didn't you reach out to me?"*

Debbie's response is devastating to Diana, *"Everyone knows how busy you are. I didn't want to bother you."*

The two women speak for hours. The conversation is rich, deep, and heartfelt. There is a bond between them as Diana sees Debbie as a younger version of herself.

By now, the restaurant is empty and the staff is preparing for the lunch rush. It is time to wrap things up.

Diana asks Debbie where she is going. Debbie promptly shares the name of the firm and Diana congratulates her. The firm is reputable and will be good for her career. Feeling a strong connection, Diana asks her how much the new firm will be paying her. Debbie lets her know that it is a pay raise of $6,000 and enough to afford a new apartment.

As Diana processes this information, she realizes what a shame it is to lose Debbie. She could easily afford to give Debbie a $12,000 raise and still be very profitable.

> **When considering pay raises, do you ever consider what it would cost to replace that employee?**

Diana asks Debbie if there is anything she can do to make her reconsider. In a move that makes Diana regret this loss even more, Debbie calmly declines and stresses that it is important to honor the commitment to her new firm.

It is a shame to lose such a talented employee. This problem was completely avoidable. Diana lets Debbie know how classy she believes her response to be. She then lets Debbie know that she would always be welcomed back if her new firm doesn't work out. Additionally, Diana gives Debbie her mobile phone number and lets her know that she will *never* be too busy to support her career.

Debbie concludes the conversation with the following remark: *"Thank you, Diana. I feel better. My exit interview was so abrupt— I thought I had done something wrong."*

Diana is angry and emotionally spent. As she returns to her office, a phone call from her outsourced HR partner is a welcome distraction from her own thoughts.

The compensation survey for her industry indicates rising salaries, but Diana's firm is still paying much better than industry numbers for most employees. The only spot where she is near the industry averages is at entry level positions— exactly where Debbie was. Overall, Diana's firm is at the high end of all compensation figures.

All this information is starting to make sense, but it still doesn't explain why some of her mid-level employees are demanding raises and why her management team is so detached. Clearly, there is more work to do.

Diana spends the next week speaking with employees and her managers. Her conversations provide some sobering conclusions:

- The changing job market is not the problem.
- Her employees are paid very well.
- Everyone is overworked and it is only getting worse.
- The management team still cares, but they are not making the time to listen, think, or develop staff.
- It is not worth losing more *Debbies* for what amounts to $3 per billable hour. It will cost three times that amount to replace her and far more in lost revenue.
- There is a disconnect between the "old guard" and the consultants. Unable to gain respect and engagement, mid-level employees are seeking recognition and growth through salary increases.
- The new incentive program is unintentionally prioritizing performance over people.
- Diana's leaders are good people that are managing poorly.
- Everyone thinks Diana is too busy to be bothered.

Diana remembers a saying her grandfather would always repeat… *"the buck stops here."* Harry Truman was her grandfather's favorite president because he wasn't afraid to take responsibility when things went wrong. Diana knows that this all falls on her shoulders, but she still has no idea what she needs to do differently.

# 12
## PROFITABILITY

Profitability seems like such an easy business concept to evaluate. If your revenues exceed your spending, you are profitable. Simple.

And while this simple formula may be very accurate, it provides no insight into the vast array of scenarios that drive profitability within an organization. Making the situation even more complex is the fact that profitability issues can be just as profound when a company is growing as well as when the organization is in decline.

Additionally, profitability issues become even more complicated because their severity accelerates at the edges of success and failure. What this means is that companies that are struggling tend to have more problems the more they struggle. Similarly, companies that are growing tend to have more problems the faster they grow. In either of these extreme situations, profitability tends to be a casualty of the compounding effects of co-dependent inputs.

All these unique characteristics make profitability an interesting area of business study. However, conventional thinking often casts unprofitability as a business problem and profitability as a solution. Profitability is neither a problem nor a solution. Profitability is a measured outcome.

Profitability is a wide-ranging business outcome the same way that fatigue is a sweeping medical symptom. Individuals with sedentary lifestyles, weak immune systems, and poor nutrition often suffer from fatigue. At the opposite end of the spectrum, very active people can eat healthy and still be fatigued because they are burning the candle at both ends. Just like profitability, fatigue accelerates at the extremes. In this regard, profitability is an outcome that presents itself as a symptom of underlying business problems.

For simplicity, our analysis will categorize symptomatic profitability into three flavors: **Severe**, **Moderate**, and **High-Class**.

## Severe

Nobody ever says they are having severe profitability issues. What you typically hear is: "we are losing money." The additional characteristic that makes the situation severe is when **compounding dependencies** create a downward performance spiral.

For example– a company with declining sales will suffer from decreasing revenues which will lead to a weaker cash position. As the strength of cash flows degrade, the ability to cover fixed expenses becomes more difficult, negatively affecting profitability. Cost cutting measures further restrict an organization's ability to service existing clients and respond to the root causes of underlying problems. Ultimately, each well-intentioned subsequent decision is often the least bad option. As has been witnessed countless times, it is very easy to let a series of small adjustments increase the challenge associated with decreasing profits.

Regardless of the situation, addressing severe profitability as a math problem is typically an accelerant to failure. It takes great courage and unconventional thinking to escape a downward profitability spiral. At a time when cost cutting seems sensible, the situation may require additional investment to develop new marketing channels and sales opportunities (Joly, 2021). In other cases, intentionally decreasing revenues by getting rid of less profitable clients and products may be the counterintuitive best path forward.

The courage associated with solving severe profitability issues is to avoid looking at profitability as the problem that needs to be solved. The key is to look at profitability as a symptom of a deeper problem. Only when the core problem is understood can the correct and seemingly unconventional solution make sense.

The core problems behind severe profitability issues can range from an inability to hire or retain workers, aging receivables, a lack of focus, slow responses to market contractions, inefficient processes, an incorrect business model, and of course, sales. Naturally, problems may be due to many of these issues at the same time or even issues that were not mentioned. The key point, however, is that profitability is not the issue. Profitability is the symptomatic outcome of deeper issues.

## Moderate

Like any Pareto distribution, most profitability issues are considered moderate because they tend to be isolated and temporary if addressed promptly. Moderate issues typically surface with comments like:"we're working harder than ever, *but* we just don't seem to have much money left at the end of the month." The common theme associated with moderate profitability issues is a lack of **discipline**.

A classic example would be a lack of discipline in expense management. It's easy to feel good when you are making money and sometimes spending can get out of hand. Of course, everyone in the office needs a new chair. Of course, we can hold our executive meetings in Hawaii this year. Of course, we can finally do that thing we've been putting off. Expense controls are a matter of discipline.

Another example would be an opportunistic sales focus that prioritizes anyone willing to purchase over the discipline of staying within product or pricing sweet spots. Sticking to what you do well every time is a profitable strategy. Straying from what you do well every time is a recipe that invites the types of inefficiencies that degrade profitability.

Yet another example would be an undisciplined sales process that prospects heavily in one quarter and then stops prospecting because they are busy closing deals and tending to client implementations. A disciplined sales team is always prospecting and filling the top of the proverbial sales funnel. When this discipline is lost because "we got too busy," sales forecasts adopt a sine wave profile that is bad for profitability.

This is not to say all moderate profitability issues are because of a lack of discipline. Some moderate issues are short-term bumps in the road. A good example of this is when fuel prices spike because a refinery is shut down after a hurricane. Unexpected events will always happen and can have short-term impacts on profitability. Even then, the companies that deliver profits on a more consistent basis are the same ones that exhibit the discipline to prepare for unexpected events.

## High-Class

If you are going to have an extreme profitability problem, high-class problems are the ones you would prefer to have. If your company's profitability is declining because you are growing too fast… you have high-class problems. If your profitability issues are tied to capital constraints because your customers have placed too many orders… you have high-class problems. It's good to have high-class problems.

There are two important commonalities with high-class profitability issues. First, they occur when everything is going great and business is booming. The second commonality is that the root cause is typically **structural** in nature. What this means is that declines in profitability begin to surface after internal processes are put under strain.

Perhaps the most common problem with high-class profitability is when cash is constrained. A flood of new orders can create the need for additional investments in capital equipment, raw materials, and talent in order to satisfy demand. All these expenditures will eventually produce more profit, but in the short-term, profitability suffers. Overtime may temporarily satisfy demand, but the premium can affect profits and quality if long-term scalability is not addressed. Additional capital to support these investments must be acquired in the form of loans or other investment vehicles that eat into normal profit margins.

A twist on this classic example is when broad increases in market demand create shortages of supply-side resources affecting the costs of production. Whether the shortage is for 304 stainless steel or Python programmers, the price to obtain raw materials or hire talent goes up. Further exacerbating the profitability challenge is the fact that additional fees such as expedited freight or signing bonuses degrade the best efforts to support existing profit levels. And while some price increases can be passed on to customers, that process frequently lags the investments necessary to keep pace with market demands.

As is the case, profitability problems increase exponentially at the extremes. It is not uncommon to see your business boom at the same time everyone else's business is booming. And then, all these scenarios can feed on one another as the strain of success envelops an organization.

■ ■ ■

Running a business is a tireless affair. But the freedom of being your own boss and doing things your own way comes at a price. And the price of entrepreneurship includes business requirements that shackle you to boring functions like accounting, insurance, and taxes. It's the part of business that Diana hates the most.

On this particular day, Diana is having her monthly financial review with the company controller. She gets weekly status reports, but the monthly review is a face-to-face meeting where she can ask questions and dive deeper into issues.

For the past several years, these meetings have been very enjoyable. The company has been growing, profits have been accumulating and the company has been financially strong. In fact, Diana stopped renting office space and purchased her own building a few years ago. Few things make Diana feel more accomplished than seeing her company's name proudly displayed above the front entrance.

> ### *Have you made any purchases to satisfy your vanity?*

As the meeting kicks off, the controller has an uneasy look on his face. He starts by saying that billings have been declining in recent weeks due to some of the employee departures. He further explains that this wouldn't have been a big problem in years past. The main expense with their service business is salary and benefits, variable expenses that track well with headcount. But now that they own the building, the situation has changed.

The problem is that the business now has much higher fixed costs due to the mortgage on the building. Diana's business was so profitable that she chose to go with a 15-year mortgage instead of a longer term. This raised her monthly expenses, but it was appealing because she would eventually own her building outright and then have no payments– right about the time the twins would be headed to college.

The mortgage also came with a few bank covenants, rules the bank gives that govern what she can or can't do while paying down her debt. One of those covenants is to keep a sizable balance in her business checking account.

Diana has always had a decent line of credit to handle clients that habitually paid on longer terms such as Net 90. There was at least one client project each year that jammed up the cash flow such that the line of credit became important for payroll. This year, the late payer is Diana's largest client.

The timing of all these events, coupled with the banking restrictions, has created an unexpected cash crisis. Payroll is due. The mortgage is due. Estimated tax payments are due. On top of that, she has dipped into her business account and her line of credit deep enough to be nearing some of the bank covenants. If the covenants kick-in, the interest rate on her loan will increase… only making her problems worse.

Diana's business is profitable, but the threshold for a crisis is much lower than it used to be. The small dip in profitability due to decreased billings has been enough to create a perfect storm of financial stress.

> *Have you ever experienced a financial storm?*

After a lengthy discussion, they arrive at a workable plan. If Diana can forgo salary for a few months and they accept pre-negotiated early payment discounts from their largest client, they will be back on track in three months.

This whole process has exhausted Diana. Fortunately, she can promptly address the issues and get her business back on track. With a bit of financial discipline, she will be able to create a cushion that will make the business much less sensitive to fluctuations in profitability. Diana is thankful that she has what many would consider high-class problems.

# 13

## GROWTH

As a child, growing pains are considered a painful inconvenience. We have no control over them, and they are an unavoidable part of growing up. It is a mistake, however, to view business growing pains in the same light. Business growth issues are a privilege.

In the world of business, growth is a fascinating topic of study. It is often mistaken for a strategy, but it is not. It is also mistaken as a solution, but it is not. Growth is an outcome of aligned business strategies and tactics much like culture is an outcome of an organization's daily decisions.

Growth issues are so interesting because they deal with the delicate balance of the rate of change within a business. And regardless of the source, change is never a comfortable proposition. Unbridled growth can be difficult to manage and frequently spawns additional issues. Stagnant growth can signal oversights in business models and strategy, while steady growth is the sign of a well-run business. A close evaluation of growing pains will highlight the **constraints** that limit a business from achieving its optimal potential.

Growing pains come in many varieties that correlate with their underlying constraints. The most common varieties are related to operations, business models, resources and sales.

# Operations

The best metaphor for understanding operational scaling issues is something everyone is familiar with– cooking. Imagine the effort to cook steaks on the grill for a family of four. All four steaks would fit on the grill at the same time, so it is possible to have all of them finished at the same time so everyone can eat together. However, if we had to cook steaks for 250 people at a gathering, the problem would be much more complex. How would we ensure that everyone gets a warm and juicy steak at a similar time?

This is similar to the problem experienced by Harlan Sanders, founder of Kentucky Fried Chicken. His roadside restaurant was famous for tasty fried chicken. However, the time to cook each entree was thirty to forty minutes– too long for road weary travelers to wait. In an effort to satisfy a growing demand for his product, Harlan Sanders had to rethink how he went about cooking his chicken. After much research and testing, he replaced his original method with pressure cookers and reduced cooking time to nine minutes.

This innovation resolved one of the key constraints that was preventing Kentucky Fried Chicken from scaling as a burgeoning fast-food enterprise.

# Business Model

The pressure cooker innovation helped Harlan Sanders run his operation in a manner that maximized throughput for his roadside restaurant. But when the new interstate highway system moved traffic away from his location, the business suffered. This event was the catalyst that exposed the second constraint on the growth of Colonel Sander's enterprise: the ability to fund expansion into additional locations.

As his business suffered a decrease in revenue, Sanders was constrained from moving to a new location to survive. Additionally, at 62 years of age, it would be difficult for Harlan Sanders to make his mark on the world by cash flowing a slow growth model one restaurant at a time. To resolve this constraint, he cleverly adopted a franchising model that fueled the growth of his business.

Initially, the franchising model allowed Kentucky Fried Chicken to be added to the menu of already successful restaurants throughout the United States. This business model was a low cost and low risk way to grow the brand and generate revenues from the unique value proposition pioneered by Harlan Sanders– delicious fried chicken in nine minutes.

Eventually, Kentucky Fried Chicken was not just a menu item at other restaurants, it became the entire menu for dedicated franchises. The change in business model allowed KFC to become the international sensation we know today with over twenty-four thousand locations worldwide.

## Resources

One of the great constraints to the growth of any business or industry can be the scarcity of critical resources. These resources can be materials such as lumber for home construction, rare earth metals for semiconductors or even affordable capital in the form of loans, lines of credit, or private/public investment options. Any of these shortages can trigger industry-wide constraints on growth and profitability.

In other cases, specialty materials like 304 stainless steel, or people with particular skills, like Python programmers, can be unique to a specific product design or company. In these latter two instances, the type of steel or programming language were chosen for specific reasons that might not have considered growth.

Stainless steel may have been chosen for corrosion resistance, but a regular carbon steel that is plated to protect from corrosion may be a suitable replacement that is in greater supply and a better choice to support growth.

More specifically, the selection of a programming language may be based on personal preferences or recommendations of software architects. However, if growth were factored into the technology strategy, other programming language choices may provide access to a more abundant supply of programmers at a more affordable cost.

Growth constraints can often be tied to decisions that were made to optimize a situation at a point in time instead of support- ing a business strategy that changes as a firm grows. Some of these decisions are necessary waypoints in the evolution of a product and/or service while others are oversights that never considered growth.

## Sales

All sales are not equal. The process to achieve one million in reve- nue is different from the process to hit the ten million mark. And once you achieve ten million in revenue the process to cross over to fifty million is yet again different. As businesses grow, it is inevitable that inflection points are reached where the approach must change, and processes must be updated for growth to continue.

A common inflection point is tied to the cost of sales (CoS). When companies are smaller, an inefficient sales model can mask the many non-sales personnel that contribute to each sales effort. Founders, CEOs, and executives are often involved in every sale in order to close deals. While this may improve close rates, it is a recipe that does not scale. As the company grows, the sales process eventually breaks down.

And this problem frequently gets worse. As the sales process is broken down and evaluated it may be revealed that a product is so complex that a single sale requires too much technical and industry knowledge. In other scenarios, the product is being sold to an industry/market base that is too broad to concentrate the necessary efforts and spending to scale efficiently. Regardless, the resulting high cost of sales reveals a product that needs to be retooled or repositioned in the market for a profitable growth trajectory.

At the other end of the spectrum, companies that enjoy a surplus of sales may find that it is more profitable to raise prices than increase the strain on operations to deliver the product or service the company offers. Unfortunately, this revelation does not typically occur until operational growing pains become pronounced and quality begins to suffer.

Constraints have an interesting way of showing up in sales processes. Whether it is access to "closers" with deep product knowledge, high selling costs, or pricing that is not in line with demand, sales related issues happen at many critical inflection points in the developmental arc of a business.

■ ■ ■

Growing the business was tough when it was small and getting started, but nobody told Diana how difficult it would be to manage growth when the business was flourishing. Until recently, everything seemed like it was going along just fine. Her team was capable, she was hiring top young talent, her finances were strong, and her reputation was growing even stronger.

In recent years, Diana wasn't even struggling with sales. Either she had gotten much better at selling or the market demand was high for her services. Perhaps it was both. Regardless of the rationale, business has been booming.

Her desire to grow the business was never about making more money, but rather, to grow acceptance that environmentally sound business practices could also be more profitable business practices. This mission has fueled and fulfilled Diana and her team.

Naturally, the burden of additional projects required more coordination and focus from her leadership team. Diana thought she saw some of this coming and did her best to prepare. The new incentive program was designed to balance workloads and motivate people to work through the strain of onboarding new clients and talent. It seemed to be working... at least for a while.

Now, Diana feels like the wheels have come off the bus. The incentive program feels like a disaster, talented consultants are leaving the organization, and collaboration within her teams is at an all-time low. On top of that, Diana is starting to see the strain on her team affect important client relationships she has worked tirelessly to build.

After investing so much of her heart and soul into this business, these problems were not the reward she had anticipated. She has always treated her people well. Her clients have always revered the professionalism and dedication of her team. And within the industry, Diana is exceptionally well respected.

How then is her growing business short on cash and hemorrhaging people? How is it that success means she can't take a salary from her own firm? Why does success taste so bitter?

---

> ### *Have you endured the bitter tastes of success?*

---

Emotionally, Diana feels as though she is at a low point exactly when she should have been at a high point. Nothing feels good. Nothing is stable. Nothing is comfortable.

And while Diana knows that foregoing salary for a few months is the correct thing to do as a leader, she personally resents the fact that her team could have avoided this whole situation if they had just been doing what they were supposed to do. Diana feels guilty for thinking this, but she can't ignore her strong feelings of betrayal and resentment.

> *Have you ever felt betrayed by your team?*

Diana is deep into a pity party when the phone rings. It is her mother-in-law.

Contrary to the stereotype, Diana's mother-in-law is a wonderful supporter and an inspiration to her. She always has a kind word and a thoughtful perspective that portrays the world in a better light. The clarity of her thinking and her loving support are just what the doctor ordered.

Diana spends a few minutes explaining her situation while her mother-in-law listens carefully. Even though Diana would love to have someone tell her what to do, she appreciates the fact that her mother-in-law just listens and asks questions. What is deeply comforting is that her questions are all born from a natural curiosity. It is clear that her mother-in-law is genuinely invested in understanding Diana's plight and not just placating her emotional venting.

Diana has always admired this about Dean's mother. She is an amazing woman with a capacity to connect with other people in a way that is sincere and heartfelt. Her questions evoke thoughtful introspection and never feel like an inquisition. Conversations with her mother-in-law always calm Diana's nerves and help her feel more confident.

Her mother-in-law may not be an expert in environmental consulting, but anyone she interacts with quickly recognizes how well she understands people and human nature. This is exactly the type of support Diana needs right now.

*"Diana, honey, we're all so proud of you and your accomplishments. Everyone admires you for the challenges you've taken on and overcome. Why are you expecting things to be easy when you've never chosen the easy path?"*

It's a good question that leaves Diana speechless. Her mother-in-law is right.

*"But why does it seem like the sacrifices and the challenges keep getting bigger and more difficult. Shouldn't everything be getting easier?,"* Diana replies.

*"Diana, dear… I remember what it was like when we first came to America. We didn't have much. It is easy to go without when you have nothing, but it is harder to go without when you have everything. Be thankful for all that you have. The depth of your sacrifice is a measure of how much you have achieved. Don't let these setbacks cloud your vision and your greater purpose. Your determination and persistence have fueled all of your success… why would you want to abandon that now?"*

Diana looks over at the clock and realizes they have been talking for over an hour. With just a few great questions and comments, her mother-in-law has refreshed and focused her mind. More importantly her emotions are in-check, and she can appreciate all the good that has come from her hard work.

# 14

## DIANA'S EPIPHANY

If running a company and working around her husband's hectic surgical schedule weren't enough, Diana is a dedicated mother to five-year-old twins.

On a particularly busy Thursday afternoon, Diana is juggling some lingering deliverables from work, planning for dinner, and corralling her highly energetic twins. Her husband, Dean, will be busy with his E-R trauma shift well into Friday. It is a tough way to finish out the work week, but it is the life they chose.

Diana knows how fortunate she is to "have it all." They have been blessed with a girl and a boy who are healthy and curious about the world around them. On top of that, Diana is grateful that her team understands how important it is for her to work from home when Dean is on call.

Even then, five-year-old twins can still test your nerves.

From the playroom off her home office, Diana hears the faint whimper of *"Mom-eeeee"* that signals her presence is required. As she turns the corner and enters the playroom, she wades into an ankle-deep sea of brightly colored plastic toys. The toy shelves are completely empty and she wonders how this could happen so quickly after she cleaned up just a few hours ago.

Her daughter is distraught. The fifth family member, a stuffed animal named Doggie, is nowhere to be found. The situation is not yet critical, but it is close. The children said they were looking for Doggie, but they could not find him. Perhaps Mom can help expedite the process.

This is the last thing Diana needs at the end of a stressful week. She is alone and dealing with work deadlines, employee issues, as well as dinner. How is it that all these toys could be on the floor in such a short period of time? Don't the kids know that they would have no problem finding Doggie if they just put their toys away after they finished playing with them? Why is this such a difficult proposition?

At the peak of her frustration, she has a parental epiphany.

What if the way to look for a specific toy was to not look for that specific toy? What if the way to look for a toy was to pick up and put away every toy that was *not* the one you were looking for? Pretty soon we wouldn't have the distractions of all the other toys, and it would be easier to find the toy we were seeking.

It was a novel approach. She explained it to the twins and described it as a game: *"The faster we put away the toys that are not Doggie... the faster we can find Doggie. And the winner will get to pick what we have for dinner."* It was a longshot, but it was worth a try.

To her surprise and delight, the new strategy worked remarkably well. After half of the clutter was off the floor and where it belonged on the shelves, Doggie's soiled face smiled up at her daughter and averted further crisis. The only part of the plan that backfired was that dinner was processed dinosaur chicken nuggets and tater tots… again.

A few hours after dinner, the kids were ready for bed and so was Diana. It was a long week and tomorrow promised to be a challenging day. Relaxing on the sofa Diana reflected on her toy searching epiphany and couldn't wait to tell Dean.

Shortly after she put the kids to bed, she returned to the sofa and instinctively opened up her laptop to work. She stared at the screen blankly with no clear direction or motivation for what she was doing. It was a long day and her cognitive energy was spent. Why did she even open her laptop?

Something was nagging at her. Diana knew that the longer she delays dealing with the problems her business is facing, the worse the problems will get. It has been over a month since she started noticing the cracks in the foundation of her business. Surely, by now, she should have been able to find the problem.

After a moment of self-pity, she laughs out loud realizing that the answer has been right there in the playroom all day. She is looking for the problem in the same way her children were looking for Doggie.

What if she started figuring out what was *not* the problem? Would the answer jump out at her and stare her in the face like Doggie did for her daughter?

Her realization is comforting and exhausting at the same time. It has been a long day and a long week. Diana seeds her mind with this thought and decides to tackle the issue first thing in the morning.

It was rare for Diana to wake up before her alarm. They often joked that her relationship with the snooze button was nearly as important to her as her relationship with Dean. On this day, however, Diana was up, awake, and excited to take on the day. She was refreshed and energized with a new approach to solving her most important problem.

Diana reviewed the last month and her painstaking evaluation of what was plaguing her business. She realizes that much of what she has concentrated on are symptoms of larger problems. She needs to find the core issues that are surfacing symptomatic problems such as turnover and conflict within her organization.

Unless having too many sales is an issue, that is not her problem right now. And since sales are so strong, she knows her services are in high demand. Scaling might be an issue, but it is hardly driving all the issues with accountability and alignment that her business is facing. Her pricing is also at the high end of the spectrum, so she is confident that her positioning in the marketplace is solid.

Furthermore, Diana's company has a strong line of credit, so the short-term cash flow issues are not as threatening as they feel. Even with the rash of salary increases she is facing; the business model is highly profitable so there is no need to think that profitability is the core issue facing the business.

Diana takes a step back from this process and realizes she has already put a bunch of "toys" away. This energizes her to push forward with the process.

---

### *What "toys" can you put away?*

---

Could the problem be focus? It does seem as though people are going in different directions. This could be the type of issue that would lead to many of the problems the organization is experiencing. A lack of coordinated focus would explain a lot. The process is working!

Perhaps it is the people. Does she have the wrong people in her organization? She does have conflict and a fair amount of personal agency and expectation management issues. The thought terrifies her. Diana loves her people and can't bear to think that, for her company to grow, she might have to let go of people she regards as family.

Diana questions her strategy and the incentive program that has been received so poorly. How could it be the strategy? It addresses all the key issues plaguing her team and the growth of the business. The strategy is mindful, scalable, and sound. Perhaps the strategy is good, but her leaders implemented it poorly. Could that be the problem?

It is still early in the morning and at least an hour has passed. Diana knows that the day will get into full swing shortly and that she has precious few moments to get herself ready before the twins awaken.

As she checks her hair in the mirror, she gets a good look at herself. At that moment, she does not see her own reflection. She sees a woman named Diana. And just as her daughter found Doggie staring up at her, Diana sees the core problem of her business staring her in the face. The common thread in everything is her. Diana's leadership, or lack thereof, is the reason her company is dealing with issues of focus, alignment, turnover, and conflict.

As she stares this person in the face, she realizes she was out scouting new pastures and focusing so much on the future, that she had stopped tending to her own flock. She thought she had been so successful delegating that she had no role to play in the day-to-day operations of her business. She was dead wrong. Diana needed to re-engage in her business as the leader and not as an observer.

Somewhat satisfied with her epiphany, Diana is comforted that the core issue –her leadership– has been identified. But perhaps the most important outcome is Diana's realization that identifying the core problem is only the first step toward a clear path forward and a brighter future.

# PART II

## IDENTIFYING CORE PROBLEMS & SKILLS

It was late 1999 and the dot.com boom was nearing the peak of its irrational exuberance. My wife Dana and I were expecting our first child in early March, and we were excited to be parents. My full-time job had me traveling to Atlanta every week and my successful side-hustle Internet startup was filling every evening. It was an exciting and stressful time.

The phone rang late one afternoon, and I welcomed the always cheerful voice of my cousin, Bob: *"Jimmy! How are you?"*

A recruiter friend of Bob's had asked him if he knew of anyone for a role he was trying to fill. Bob said that he immediately thought of me. He described the situation and how it would require a relocation back to Chicago. The timing was perfect to exit my profitable startup, stop traveling and get closer to family. It seemed like divine intervention. Yes! I was interested.

It was a great time to be negotiating for new positions. Internet jobs were hard to fill, and they also commanded top dollar. Everything was falling into place. I negotiated a deal with my business partner, told my friends I would be moving, put the house on the market, and got set to move back to Chicago. When they heard the news, my parents were elated.

I was very grateful that my employer at the time and my new company both honored our request to delay my transition by four weeks until after my son was born. It was a classy move by both organizations.

But those were not just any four weeks - it was the four weeks when the dot.com bubble burst. There was a flurry of activity on my first day of work, just two weeks after my son was born. It was not the good kind of busy. The firm I had joined had just finished huge Y2K projects and had literally hundreds of consultants that were "on the bench." I was the "Internet guy" and was supposed to help bring a new type of work into the business. The bursting of the bubble pretty much killed that idea.

Panic set in. I was a new father. I just left a comfortable world. My house was on the market. I said goodbye to my closest friends. What did I just do?

There was no escape. There were no other jobs. There was no going back. The ships had been burned.

With my back to the wall, I set my mind to working hard and doing whatever it took to survive. My wonderful wife Dana understood the situation and ensured that I could enjoy treasured family moments in the small pockets of time when I was not working. Failure was not an option.

The next five years were perhaps the most intense work experience I would ever face for the remainder of my career. Our company experienced just about every problem a business could encounter. As consultants and members of an industry that was unraveling, we were able to observe and experience a concentration of existential business problems that was unprecedented in recent times.

School was in session. Anyone who was paying attention could experience more and learn more than any other time in their careers. I was grateful to have the context of my Marquette MBA to put many of these learnings into context. The hidden opportunity in this crisis was not lost on me.

The implosion of the dot.com bubble allowed several things to become abundantly clear:

- People hastily treat symptoms instead of problems.
- Core business problems fall into predictable buckets.
- Acquiring a skill does not solve a business problem.
- People often value activity over achievement.
- Exigent circumstances can clarify thinking.
- Opportunities lie in the problems everyone is having.

This section is dedicated to the understanding of core business problems and the discipline necessary to find clarity when a crisis is not there to focus your mind.

# 15

## CASE STUDY – SAM

Sam is the vice president of sales for a software company. He has led large software sales teams in the past with great success. His new firm is backed by substantial venture capital and is poised to grow wildly over the next several years. This is an exciting opportunity for Sam. He has made good money in the past, but this is the first time he has been able to get an ownership stake in a firm through generous stock grants. Sam has always helped other people get rich and now he believes it is his turn to capitalize on the sales growth he is known to deliver.

In fact, Sam was so confident in his abilities that he invested some of his own money into the company during their last funding round. What was notable about his investment is that he made it before he formally took over from the prior sales leader he was replacing. Sam's wife Sarah is also confident in her husband and his talents, but she was reluctant to invest so much money in a company after working so hard to establish a comfortable lifestyle for their family. Sam has a lot riding on the success of this company.

Sam was brought into this company because revenue growth had stalled out. Eager to ensure the success of their investment, the venture capital firm encouraged company leadership to consider a more experienced software sales leader. Sam was one of several experienced leaders that the company had courted and was chosen because of his back-to-basics sales management philosophy.

When Sam took over, the sales team was feeling overworked and not accountable for the lack of results. To compound the challenge, several of the most experienced sales personnel left to join other startups only days after he started. None of these challenges fazed Sam. He was confident that good discipline and an increased focus on the basics is all that this company needed. This was a winning recipe that worked well for Sam before, and he was confident that it would work again.

Sam was originally attracted to this company because of the amazing software product. The founders of the company came up with an innovative way to combine complex business modeling capabilities with artificial intelligence. This combination allows the software to model and forecast all kinds of business scenarios that are constantly changing. It can work for logistics, supply-chains, raw material purchasing, and even, sales forecasting.

As far as Sam is concerned, one of the most attractive aspects of this software is that it can solve just about any business problem. From his perspective, this is an easy product to sell. In fact, Sam has a hard time thinking of people and companies that would not benefit from this software. Further bolstering his confidence is the investment from the prominent venture capital firm and other notable investors. This opportunity is a sure thing.

Now that he is at the helm of the sales organization, Sam's focus is to assess his team and grow revenue by getting back-to-basics.

---

*What do you think of Sam's analysis?*
*What questions would you want to ask Sam?*
*Have you ever experienced a business opportunity*
*you thought was a sure thing?*

# 16

## DON'T JUMP!

The shortest path between two points is a straight line. It is a simple rule we learn in our youth and carry with us throughout our lives. But the shortest route is not always the fastest choice or the safest option. Our vehicle GPS systems will often redirect us on seemingly bizarre detours to help us arrive at our destination on time. Mountain climbers will rarely take the most direct route, opting instead for safer and more circuitous ascents. Regardless of the situation, the best path forward always requires the consideration of additional inputs, such as safety and time, that can be easy to ignore.

As humans, however, we often ignore additional inputs because we have a natural preference for instinctual simplicity. In Daniel Kahneman's book, *Thinking, Fast and Slow*, he outlines two modes of thinking that explain how we respond to the world around us. System 1 is fast, intuitive, and effortless. It is estimated that roughly ninety-five percent of our daily decisions are made using System 1. From an anthropological standpoint, our success as a species has relied upon human instincts that quickly recognize the threat posed by a lion or the danger of ingesting food that smells as if it has spoiled. As advanced as our society has become, our primitive brain has changed little since our ancestral origins.

In some instances, a simple conclusion we draw through System 1 is indeed the best solution to a problem. In other instances, our natural impulses can deceptively mask inputs, facts and truths which escape our attention and guide us into trouble.

When we use System 1, we are rewarded with a dopamine hit that improves our mood and provides a comforting level of satisfaction with our decision. System 2, however, is slow, intentional, and exhausting. When we invoke System 2, we leverage our analytical prefrontal cortex to examine additional inputs and much more data. It is with System 2 that we apply the logic that has allowed us to advance our society to standards of living that have even outpaced the sophistication of our own brains. Unlike System 1, though, there is no dopamine hit when we invoke System 2. The reward for using System 2 is fatigue and exhaustion coupled with a modest improvement in the accuracy of our analysis. It is no wonder that we routinely favor System 1 for much of our decision making.

Further complicating our ability to consider the full spectrum of inputs in our decision making is the stress of our daily lives. In times of stress, we are hardwired to narrow our perspective and limit our inputs. This stress response is well-studied and predictable (Yu, 2016). Under stress, our minds do not only bias toward System 1 thinking, they are also affected by our mood. As such, we do not get our best results when stress has soured our mood and limited our thinking. And when we narrow our perspective and decline the opportunity to consider other inputs, we often jump to conclusions that do not serve us well.

The thought process we use when we jump to conclusions is hardly sophisticated enough to encompass root cause analysis or the proper assignment of correlation vs. causality. As such, we often end up treating symptoms rather than solving problems. The principal value of any rush to judgment is the emotional satisfaction of having done something.

A type of conclusion that is frequently, and hastily, drawn in business contexts is that problems are due to deficiencies in a particular skill. Our sales are lagging… we must need sales training. We are all way too busy… we must need time management or delegation training. Our people aren't collaborating effectively… we must need teamwork training.

Skills training is like the aspirin of the medicine cabinet— handy remedies that quickly treat a multitude of symptoms. New or enhanced skills may make a problem less painful or even mask a problem festering behind the scenes, but they do not inherently solve many of the core problems we face in business. We fool ourselves into thinking the acquisition of a new skill, or training our teams, solves the actual problem.

Some of the common skills we like to stock our business "medicine cabinet" with are:

| | |
|---|---|
| Teamwork | Effective Communication |
| Negotiation | Time Management |
| Sales | Delegation |
| Hiring | Conflict Management |
| Leadership | Change Management |

This is not an indictment of skills training. Skills training is an essential component of improving the performance of any organization. What this is, however, is a rejection of the hasty conclusion that new or improved skills will magically address the core issues facing any business. Skills training will help an organization that does not have underlying issues improve their performance. And for organizations with deeper problems, skills training can buy the time and space necessary to address underlying issues.

When we find ourselves reaching into the skills medicine cabinet, there is one singular word that has the power to get us closer to the core problems we face... WHY?

- Why do we need training on this skill?
- Why are we struggling with negotiation?
- Why do we believe our teamwork could improve?
- Why has communication become a problem?
- Why do we avoid difficult conversations?
- Why do we need sales training?
- Why is it that we delegate so poorly?

Consider this line of Socratic questioning that takes very little time and engages our minds in a manner that will begin to sharpen the focus on the core problem.

---

**Why do we need training in time management?**
*Because we are struggling with time management.*

**Why are we struggling with time management?**
*Because we don't have time to get anything done.*

**Why don't we have any time to get anything done?**
*Because we spend our whole day in meetings.*

**Why do we spend our whole day in meetings?**
*Because we need to keep everyone abreast of all
the projects we have going on...*

---

We could continue this line of questioning further, but it is instructive to think about where this line of questioning may terminate. Is the problem really time management or do we have too many active projects? The problem could be one of prioritization.

The problem could also be a lack of skill running effective meetings. It is not out of the question that the problem could potentially be tied to micromanagement or perhaps even a lack of trust between functional departments. Regardless of the scenario, simple Socratic questioning can slow an impulsive jump to conclusions and lead us to a clearer understanding of the core problem.

■ ■ ■

On his first day, Sam is eager to get an overview of the sales pipeline and any activity that may lead to a new client and an uptick in sales. In Sam's mind, there is no better way to start than with a win.

As he pours through the sales activity with his management team, Sam is astounded by the sheer number of open sales opportunities that are being pursued. With sales growth stalled out under his predecessor's regime, Sam did not expect to see this volume of activity registered in the CRM system. Pondering the situation, however, Sam skeptically concludes that the pipeline opportunities were artificially inflated to appease doubtful board members and investors.

Sam's management team seems solid. They are all good people with a proven history of success. If the board had confidence in the pipeline numbers, any one of his directors could have easily filled the VP role Sam now holds.

But something is not adding up in Sam's mind. His management team is good, but the sales pipeline and activity appear to be fake. With a pipeline this robust, sales should be much higher. Sam boldly asks his management team to level with him about the "reality" of the sales pipeline.

The answer he gets back is disheartening. To a person, his management team affirms that it is all real. Sam can't believe what he is hearing. An impulse of skepticism dominates his thoughts as doubts about his management team take root. Are they fearful of retribution? Are they in on some ruse to inflate the pipeline? Are they still loyal to their old boss? Are they incompetent? Why would they continue this narrative that must be false?

Perhaps this is why Sam was brought in to take over sales. Is he supposed to clean house? Is this why the board loved his back-to-basics approach?

Now angered, Sam presses his leaders on the activity levels of the sales team. Surely, with this much activity, more sales should be closing. The response he gets is again discouraging. The leadership team confirms that the salespeople are working hard and registering their activity properly in the CRM system.

Sam is conflicted. His gut instincts are telling him to trust his team, but his skepticism does not trust the data. As he tries to logically evaluate the situation, he believes that either the data is wrong, or his leaders are incapable. He struggles to imagine a scenario where the data could be correct and his leaders are being honest with him.

> *Can you think of a time when your gut instincts were at odds with your analytical mind?*

Sam knows he was hired to solve problems… and to solve problems you must have answers. And right on cue, Sam is hit with an inspirational idea– Training! With this much activity there should be more achievement. His back-to-basics approach will need to start with training. We don't know how to close. We aren't asking for the business. Our meetings are ineffective. With people who are willing to work hard, all we need is a bit of sales training and the flow of new business will improve.

As Sam communicates the plan to his leaders, he feels relieved. He has found the problem. Now all they need to do is train the salespeople and execute with new and improved selling skills.

# 17

## SO MANY PROBLEMS

After nearly thirty years of consulting with countless organizations, one phrase is ubiquitously uttered somewhere near the onset of each engagement– *"but our company is different."*

As a young consultant, I believed clients when they told me they were as unique as a unicorn in a gilded forest. Rightfully, each of these scenarios was new and distinct to my inexperienced eyes. After more years under my belt and exposure to a broader set of clients, I began to see trends and patterns with the business problems I encountered. The unique nature of each business became less of a reality and more of an unsubstantiated belief. I was fascinated by the striking similarities between businesses and especially across industries.

I saw my ability to draw parallels from one industry or company to another as a product of my experience and a sign of my mastery as a consultant. In many ways it was. When I brought these similarities to the attention of my clients, however, it was a rude awakening that highlighted many additional gaps in my professional understanding.

Every client wants to feel as though they are special and unique. And when you try to explain how the problem a manufacturer of pharmaceuticals is having is the same as that of a financial services firm... good luck making any progress earning their trust. Regardless of how benign, repetitive, or ordinary a problem may be, each client views their situation as unique and extraordinary.

Once I finally matured as a consultant, I never made mention of where my inspiration may have originated. The experienced consultant suggests an idea and lets the client adopt it as their own custom-tailored solution to their unique situation. There is no value in helping someone feel less special.

As a practical matter, though, our problems do tend to fall into predictable buckets that span all industries. And while this could be a topic of great debate, my years as a consultant guide me toward these nine general problem areas:

| | | |
|---|---|---|
| Sales | Pricing/Positioning | Business Model |
| People | Financial | Strategy |
| Focus | Product/Service | Leadership |

Each of these generalized problem areas are quite broad and incorporate many sub-topics of problems that one could argue are deserving of a top spot. For the sake of this book, we will not entertain that discussion. What we will do is argue that there are general categories of problems and that having "buckets" to group specific problems can be a useful method of segmenting the core issues facing any business.

One statement that nobody can argue with is that there is no perfect business. Even the companies we admire most have their share of problems. What differentiates the companies that enjoy greater success is an acknowledgment of their own faults and earnest attempts to overcome them. The tried-and-true way to improve and compete is to learn from your mistakes.

However, companies frequently seem unaware of problems in their midst. It is the rare case where negligence or malfeasance keeps a company from addressing problems within their organization. In most cases, unresolved issues are innocently overlooked or have yet to surface a degree of pain that gets the attention of company leadership.

Furthermore, many problems are overlooked because we believe we have solved them before we even fully understand them. Reactionary problem solving may occasionally address the root cause of a problem, but it is more likely that our impulsive efforts do little more than temporarily minimize the severity of the true underlying issue. This is why we need more structured methods (5 Whys, Fishbone diagrams, Six Sigma, etc.) to identify and test for true root causes. The core issues facing a business are often hidden behind layers of symptoms and dependencies that are difficult to unmask.

When you start evaluating a business issue and identifying which causal factors are contributing to the overall problem, you can uncomplicate a difficult situation in the same way that Diana helped her daughter find her missing toy. Instead of looking for one root cause, we can simplify our analysis by using these nine general problem areas to independently evaluate how each factor affects the overall situation.

What we will do in the remaining chapters of this section is succinctly define and evaluate the buckets for each of the nine main problem areas businesses face. We will also put what we've learned into the context of Sam's situation and examine the process Sam uses to identify the core issues facing his business.

It should be noted that each of these nine problem areas are worthy of an entire book dedicated to a deeper understanding and tactics for resolving specific challenges. This is not that book. This book on clarity, however, might be the one that helps you figure out where to start and which book to read next. And with that next step identified, you are closer to a clear path forward.

If you are interested in further reading and book recommendations for each of these problems, sign up for the Business Wisdom newsletter at www.businesswisdom.com.

# 18

## SALES

Anyone who thinks sales is easy has never sold for a living. Selling is a difficult and complex business process that is often misunderstood and oversimplified. People love to characterize salespeople as unskilled yet charming pseudo-professionals with limited intellect. This is true in some cases, but the same can be said for just as many bankers, managers, lawyers, and other professionals.

Sales also invites more scrutiny than other aspects of any business because it is easy to measure and the simple fact that more sales is the "cure-all" that masks most problems behind the benefit of business sustaining revenue.

Sales revenue is one of the most consistent business measures across all businesses and industries. As such, it is often treated as a result rather than the complex set of human interactions that it is. Success in sales is about relationships, trust, mutual respect, and the fair exchange of value. A portion of the sales process that is often overlooked is that it is a two-party transaction. One party is selling, and the other party is buying. We fool ourselves into believing that individual mastery of this process is solely based on improving our selling skills. What we frequently overlook, however, is that a deeper understanding of the buying process is the facet of the transaction that matters most. A sale cannot exist without a buyer, and those that understand the psychology of the buying process have an unfair advantage.

Those who excel at sales are often credited for their uncanny timing. The conditions under which someone is ready to buy can disappear as fast as they materialize. This is why patience, timing, and speed play such critical roles in the success of any sales organization. The less friction there is between the opening of the buying window and the ability to complete a transaction can make the difference between success and failure. The velocity of the sales process plays a significant role in the success of any growing organization.

Other factors within the realm of sales involve any of the support functions that bring two parties together to complete a transaction. Departments like marketing, quoting, product development, legal, and sales engineering all play roles in the tapestry of business functions needed to finalize a sale.

■ ■ ■

It has been two months since the training, and Sam is hopeful that the pipeline numbers begin to convert into closed deals. Everyone agreed that the sales training Sam coordinated for the team was fantastic. Overall, the sales professionals seem to be energized by the leadership change and the investment in their success. His team is confident, and confidence is a good baseline mentality when you are in sales.

When he looks at the numbers with his leadership team, however, Sam is not witnessing the change he had expected. The velocity of deals flowing through the sales pipeline has remained unchanged. Sam wasn't expecting a miracle, but with improved closing skills, he thought there would be some improvement in the number of deals closing each week.

Sam now has doubts about his back-to-basics approach. There have been some positive benefits from the training, but none of them have translated into an increase in sales velocity. In retrospect, it is clear to Sam that a lack of sales skill was not the core issue keeping the company's sales growth stagnant.

Sam begins to wonder if he has the wrong people in customer-facing sales roles.

> *Do you find it difficult to hire good sales professionals?*

# 19

## PEOPLE

Human beings are the most incredible, complex, and capable entities on planet earth. Our brains alone contain billions of cells and trillions of synaptic connections. But for all our marvelous capabilities, we create as many problems for ourselves as we solve.

Perhaps this is because we can be both unpredictable and predictable at the same time. We are predictable, in large part, because of the many logical biases that quietly influence our behavior in ways that rarely surface in our conscious mind. We are simultaneously unpredictable because of our imagination, our creativity, and our exceptional ability to adapt to an endless supply of stimuli. This unique juxtaposition of two opposing contexts makes individual interactions and any broader human system exceptionally difficult to comprehend, model or manage.

Regardless of how much progress we make with technologies such as artificial intelligence, it is important to remember that most of our businesses exist to serve the needs of people. As such, human beings are an essential and inextricable component of the business world.

Even though we like to vilify scapegoats and lionize heroes, it is rarely a single person that is accountable for any success or failure.

Our anthropological hegemony as a species is not a function of individual efforts, but rather, the result of cooperation across networks of interpersonal relationships.

Our most powerful and productive relationships are based on the foundations of trust, equity, respect, and empathy. And while trust is the currency of powerful relationships, listening is the most powerful tool in our arsenal to improve empathy, respect, and equity in the workplace.

Eighty percent of the symptoms identified in Section 1 directly involve people. Factors such as accountability, agency, alignment, expectations, motivation, hiring, and communication are just a few of the many challenges we face when people are involved. And the best way to diagnose any problem involving people is to ask questions and listen carefully. The clues are all there.

■ ■ ■

Sam's doubts about his people have him concerned that the turnaround may be more complicated than he initially thought. Still confident in his own abilities, Sam decides to participate in some sales calls to directly observe what is going on in the sales process. Perhaps *he* can close them.

> *Have you ever doubted your team and stepped in to show them how it's done?*

After sitting in on a few sales calls, Sam is perplexed. His sales team seems to be employing all the new techniques and strategies that were part of the sales training he coordinated. Prospects are engaged and interested, but they are still slow to commit. Sam asks many questions to identify the source of trepidation in their prospects.

There is a theme in some of the answers he is hearing from potential customers. One customer expressed it best: *"Your product is amazing and super flexible. I'm just not sure how we would use it exactly and that makes it difficult to justify the investment in both time and money. Until we figure that out, we've got other priorities that are a bit more pressing."*

Sam is comforted that prospects find their software product to be amazing. Without a good product, it doesn't matter how strong your salesforce is. But prospects only seem to commit to a purchase after long and complicated proofs of concept are conducted for their individual scenarios. He will never reach his revenue growth goals if this does not change.

> ### *Is your sales process longer than it should be?*

# 20

## PRODUCT/SERVICE

Businesses develop products and services to create value for their customers. That value may come in the form of a solution to a problem, the enhancement of an experience or the creation of a new capability. These are just a few of the creative ways in which businesses add value to our lives.

To be successful in the marketplace, the value proposition of a product must be compelling enough for people to divert money, time, and resources away from other alternatives. It would seem obvious that the most potent alternatives would be competitive products and services. Strangely, though, the most powerful alternative is almost always doing nothing.

The inertia required to change established habits and patterns of behavior is the greatest challenge any new product or service faces in the marketplace. And the greatest method to build momentum and overcome resistance is to connect emotions to the need for change.

Products and services run into problems when their value is not readily apparent, hard to explain, or difficult to quantify. If the value proposition of a product or service is not obvious, the emotional engagement necessary to move forward must first pass through a series of logic hurdles that are as daunting and time consuming as the Twelve Labors of Hercules. Without a clear path toward a materially better future, people will always avoid the promise of value for the certainty of the present state (Kahneman and Tversky, 1992).

Failures to provide or properly articulate value are the ways in which most problems occur in this space. Issues with product quality naturally affect brand value and reputation. Likewise, a sub-par service experience can overshadow superior product performance. Alternately, value that is created through innovation must be balanced such that it is sufficient to differentiate but not so foreign that it is hard to comprehend. The failure to understand a customer's challenge in perceiving value is the source of many product and service-related problems.

■ ■ ■

Sam is starting to see a different side of the sales problem. While customers do appreciate the utility of improving their decision-making capabilities, his sales team is struggling to translate that capability into scenarios that are specific enough to each customer.

The way the process works today is that sales engineers work with prospects to develop a proof of concept (PoC) that can demonstrate a specific scenario to a client with their own data. It is a complex process that is quite an effort to coordinate. And while the organization collaborates well to provide excellent results, the whole ordeal is time consuming for his company and each of the prospects. Regardless of cost, the process to show the value of his product just takes too much time.

> *Do you have a good grasp on the average length of your sales process?*

What is more of an issue is that they have a software solution that can't be sold without a service component. Sam is starting to see that his company is selling a product with an identity crisis. Is it a product or a service or both?

Perhaps the most difficult realization for Sam is that they are struggling to sell their product in a booming economy. While it didn't make much sense at first, Sam is now realizing that the great economic conditions are hurting them more than they are helping them. Most of their PoCs are focused on optimizing processes that allow companies to cut costs and operate more efficiently. This value proposition loses some of its impact when their prospective customers are enjoying the many benefits of a wonderful economy. Perhaps they are focusing on the wrong pain that their prospects are having.

Sam now realizes that it might not be wise to be everything to everyone. The incredible flexibility of the software, something Sam originally found so appealing, has become a liability. If people can't quickly identify how this product will help their business, the sales process will remain slow and cumbersome. If his team can't focus on the pains that customers are having *right now*, their ability to sell their product's value diminishes greatly. Sam is starting to accept that they need a more focused approach to speed up the sales process.

> *Does your product or service have a narrow or a broadly focused value proposition?*

# 21

## FOCUS

The tip of a spear is sharpened to a point to focus the energy of a thrust into a tiny area. This technique allows hunters to pierce through animal hides and warriors to defeat an opponent's armor. Concentrating energy in this way is an effective concept that has been in use for thousands of years.

Even more impressive is what can be accomplished by a focused mind. From the pyramids of Egypt to the moon landings, humans are at their very best when they focus their time and mental energy on a single objective. The ability to focus both time and mind is an essential component of success in sports, in business, and in life.

Why then do we struggle with focus? Why does this simple and powerful concept elude the grasp of so many?

Perhaps the reason we struggle with focus is because it accentuates chronic flaws in our relationship with time. Our past is filled with nostalgia and selective memories that overwrite pain and regret. Our futures are imagined narratives supported by lofty goals that embolden our outlook. But the present has no happy ending. The present is home to humility and harsh realities. And the present is the only time that values our focus.

Focus has one characteristic that prevents people from leveraging it more frequently: commitment. With the power to create regret and restrict possibilities, commitment is a potent barrier to focus. Commitment is a choice with embedded consequences.

Think of the anguish you experience when you pick the "wrong" line in the supermarket. Regret is a constant and powerful reminder of our choices. Rather than treat it as valuable feedback from which to learn, most people fear regret as a reminder of a poor choice. And because we don't like to be wrong and we can't predict the future, we like to keep our options open. Unfortunately, focus requires commitment. And decisions, by their very nature, restrict options. Hence, the conundrum: the most difficult decisions are when you have the most options.

■ ■ ■

Sam wonders if some of the sales talent that recently left the team may have answers to why the sales process seems to be sluggish. He finds a top performer with a great reputation that is willing to speak with him. Her insights are incredible.

She was originally attracted to the company for many of the same reasons as Sam. The product is powerful, versatile, and a new concept with great potential. She quickly developed a robust pipeline and marketing had supplied her with a steady flow of leads. Puzzled, Sam asked her why she left.

For her, it was simple… They were saying yes to everything. Marketing was generating leads from all over the place.

Furthermore, all the marketing literature was about how the product works rather than the specific problems each industry experiences.

Salespeople were given geographic territories rather than industry verticals they could learn and focus on. All the demos the sales engineers were doing were generic, leaving too much guesswork as to how a product could solve specific problems. It's hard to get people to commit when you don't speak their language and you make them do all the work of seeing how your product helps them.

But the last straw was when they started lowering the price. At that point she knew the company was operating out of desperation. They were no longer showcasing their unique value proposition. They had lost their focus. Prospects don't like desperation… and neither do great salespeople.

> *Are you excited about every sales opportunity or do you know when a prospect is not a good fit?*
>
> *Does your marketing literature focus on what you do or is it focused on the value your customers derive?*
>
> *Is a lower price your true value?*

# 22

## PRICING/POSITIONING

The ultimate measure of value is the price people are willing to pay for any good or service. But price is not an absolute value, it is a subjective measure that can vary greatly from one person to another. This is why people pay exorbitant prices for baseball cards, works of art and many other collectibles. But who is to say those prices are outrageous? Pricing is relative to the perspective of individual buyers.

We know from studies that people will pay hundreds of dollars for wine that ranks no better than a nine-dollar bottle (Plassmann, O'Doherty, Shiv, and Rangel, 2007). Is this because buyers of the expensive wine are influenced by the opinion of others or because marketers incorrectly assess the value of their nine-dollar bottle? Regardless of the rationale, pricing is a uniquely human interpretation of value that will remain fluid for as long as we remain human.

The establishment of value is influenced by many factors that are both logical and psychological. Scarcity can drive pricing higher via logical economic models of supply and demand. At the same time, fears of scarcity (e.g., pandemic toilet paper shortages) can drive panic buying which can irrationally inflate prices and precipitate actual shortages.

Sophisticated marketers understand the psychological underpinnings of how we assign value to products and services. They appreciate the power of the cognitive biases and logical fallacies that influence our behavior. They know how to invoke our emotions and tribal instincts to compel us to purchase a product. As Dr. Robert Cialdini has proven through his groundbreaking work on influence, humans are easily manipulated and influenced by skilled practitioners.

What we often overlook when establishing pricing is the incredible power of positioning. When we see people pay premium prices it is likely due to clever positioning that obscures more analytical value judgments. Product positioning is what powers the premium nature of brands such as Rolex, BMW, and Tiffany & Co.

When it comes to pricing and positioning, one iron-clad rule rings true. If value is hard to communicate and comprehend, price always becomes an obstacle.

■ ■ ■

Sam is haunted by the comments of the former sales representative he spoke with. Cutting prices to close deals is not a bad technique, but it must be done for the right reasons. Sam talks with some of his front-line people and realizes his team is cutting prices for all the wrong reasons. In some cases, prospects aren't even requesting price breaks.

Sam wonders why there is so much difficulty demonstrating and supporting the value of this truly innovative product. With something this innovative, they should be enjoying premium pricing. Then Sam recalls some of his prospective customer conversations; they are competing against doing nothing. And doing nothing can be a very viable alternative in a good economy. How can you undercut the price of doing nothing? Sam now realizes their current approach is a slow race to the bottom.

The importance of proofs of concept (PoCs) now makes sense. The PoCs are the only way to show the opportunity cost of doing nothing. Customers will not support premium pricing for a product that *might* solve a problem for them. It's not enough to show them how this product has helped people in other industries. Customers need proof that this product will solve *their* specific problems.

Complicating matters further is that an increasing number of the deals they are signing have an "out-clause" after one year instead of the multi-year contracts that are the lifeblood of any Software-as-a-Service (SaaS) company. The ability to get out of a contract early is not the end of the world for a newer SaaS startup, but it is an indicator that people are skeptical of the value they will see from their investment. What is most troubling is that these "out-clauses" are negotiated before the PoC even starts, completely ignoring the leverage they gain after a successful demonstration of the product's value.

But therein lies the problem. Contracts and PoCs are both costly and time consuming. How can they possibly embark on costly PoC without some assurances from their customers in writing? And how can customers embark on what is essentially a proof of value without some way to assert that insufficient value may have been provided?

If they don't look at this problem differently it could mean financial ruin for the company… and for Sarah and Sam!

---

*How do your customers learn to understand the value of your product or service?*

# 23

## FINANCIAL

On the surface, financial problems seem like they should be straightforward– you are either making money or you are not. The numbers don't lie. If you sell your product or service for more than it cost, you are profitable… just like the lemonade stand you might have had as a child.

In that light, it would be easy to think of financial issues as math problems that have definitive singular solutions. Nothing could be further from the truth. Financial problems can be exceptionally complex and the rules of accounting can be opaque and confusing. Whether you are valuing the cost of work-in-progress inventory or calculating the liability of potential warranty claims, improper discipline with accounting can spell big trouble. Even with disciplined accounting practices, highly profitable companies can get into trouble. When money is involved, there are always payment terms, loan covenants, insurance premiums, payrolls, and other commitments to keep you on your toes.

Few things raise emotional tensions faster than money. If you doubt this, just ask any small claims court judge for their opinion. My experience informs a belief that most financial issues occur because of assumptions, generalizations, oversights, and emotions that cloud a clear analysis of the financial situation. And while we believe we would never oversimplify our financial situations to that of a lemonade stand, it is commonplace to see financially critical decisions fall victim to a variety of unsophisticated influences.

How many times can we pack a room full of executives to discuss a client negotiation that is stuck on a $25K disagreement? When during the same meeting the value of the collective time spent is equivalent to $10K and the issue is still left unresolved. Furthermore, companies will frequently neglect the fact that the cost of acquiring a new customer to replace the one that may be lost in a contentious negotiation is nearly as high, if not higher, than the amount of the disagreement. It is far too common to see companies tripping over dollars trying to pick up pennies.

Kahneman and Tversky's Nobel Prize winning Prospect Theory (1979) explains that we instinctively weigh relative losses and gains more than the absolute value of a financial outcome. Their work provides a perfect explanation for the two prior examples. It takes tremendous discipline to quiet the emotions and biases that have a profound effect on our decision-making calculus.

■ ■ ■

Sam has always had good relationships with the Chief Financial Officers at the companies where he has worked. What CFO wouldn't like a sales leader that provided a consistent and growing source of life-giving revenue into the organization. Now that Sam is starting to look at his sales problem differently, though, he knows that the relationship with his new CFO is more important than ever.

Stephen is the hand-picked CFO of the venture capital firm funding the organization. He has worked with them several times before and is very experienced with fundraising and taking companies public. Stephen is well respected and quite wealthy from his prior successes.

Sam met Stephen during the interview process and the two of them got along well. Stephen responded well to Sam's process-oriented mind. Sam is not certain, but he believes that Stephen liked the fact that he presented a "recipe" for success. Sam's concern is that he no longer believes his original recipe is correct for the circumstances.

Sam sets up a meeting with Stephen so they can discuss his concerns and his recent observations. Sam knows how important it will be to set the proper tone with Stephen, so he thinks through his approach and questions with great care.

Stephen knows that Sam set up this meeting, but he starts the discussion with a few questions of his own. Perhaps the most difficult is a very direct question from Stephen: *"I haven't seen any increase in sales. Is this problem proving to be more than you can handle?"*

While this isn't the start to the meeting Sam had hoped for, he was ready for this type of question; *"I never expected this to be easy and I don't believe you did either. I'm learning more every day and I'm confident we'll figure out a strategy that will achieve the results you and the board are seeking. With that in mind, I was hoping you might help me with a few questions I have."*

Stephen offered up a respectful smile and acknowledged that the sales pro they hired just hit a nasty curveball in a high-pressure situation. No words were exchanged, but Stephen gestured that Sam was cleared to ask away.

> ### What was the last business curve ball you hit?

Sam is quite curious about one specific issue that ends up being very important to Software-as-a-Service (SaaS) companies: the

Client Acquisition Cost (CAC). His question is simple and important: *"What CAC did we project in our business model and where are we performing relative to our expectations?"*

Stephen is quick to respond with several charts that are very detailed. He is very pleased with their marketing results which are 20% below cost projections and producing a consistent flow of high-quality leads. In fact, at a 10% win rate they are well ahead of most SaaS conversion rates. Stephen continues with several comparison benchmarks for SaaS companies that show a very healthy 5:1 ratio of customer acquisition costs to lifetime account value for each new customer. As such, Stephen believes they are under-investing in marketing. With that said, Stephen does not believe that the current sales team can handle the additional workload. Sam agrees.

Through their discussion, Sam has noticed what he believes to be an oversight in Stephen's calculations. From Sam's perspective, the oversight is that custom PoCs seem to be part of every engagement. Sam sees these as costs of sales that need to be factored into the CAC. If the cost of the PoCs were accounted for, Sam estimates the ratio of customer acquisition costs to lifetime account value would plummet below 1:1– and that means the more they sell the more money they lose.

Selling more at a loss is not a winning strategy. You can't make up for your losses with more volume. Sam worries that their current approach is a recipe for disaster. And while he is hesitant to question Stephen's judgment, Sam asks him why the PoCs aren't being factored into the CAC.

Stephen calmly responds that they are not factored into the CAC because the PoCs happen after the contract is signed. Stephen asserts that they are a cost of goods sold (COGS) at that point. Additionally, Stephen sees these costs going away over time as their product gains more market acceptance.

Technically, Stephen may be correct, but Sam still disagrees with the comfortable 5:1 ratio that is fueling Stephen's optimism. Sam still sees each custom PoC as a necessary part of each sale. Furthermore, the lack of focus within marketing continues to generate leads from too many industries, geographies, and company sizes. There is no way their costs will subside anytime soon if each PoC must be a customized effort. What makes this problem worse is that customized PoCs are hard to predict, plan or price. All of which take time and money Sam does not have to spare.

Sam is concerned that this may be Stephen's first experience with a SaaS business model. If it is not, Sam is even more concerned that Stephen's interests for the organization do not extend past an Initial Public Offering (IPO). The venture capitalists and many of the company's executives stand to make a fortune as soon as the company is listed on the stock market.

Sam leaves his meeting with Stephen unsure if he has made any progress. Has he helped Stephen see a new perspective or has he created an adversary?

***What would you have said to Stephen?***

# 24

# BUSINESS MODEL

Countless business problems are the result of flawed business models. In fact, it is startling how many times I have encountered businesses with models that were poorly engineered, misunderstood, or just plain neglected.

A good business model is like an ecosystem. It considers important characteristics such as balance, growth, change, resources, and renewal. A properly constructed business model will examine all these factors as both constraints and sources of growth. Moreover, a sound business model will mimic three important qualities of healthy ecosystems we observe in nature– **efficiency**, **repeatability**, and **resilience**.

A sustainable business model must be efficient in its use of resources. Two of the most constrained resources a healthy business requires are people and money. Few businesses ever get to the point where they have sufficient amounts of either to satisfy their needs. Accordingly, critical resources can both fuel and limit the success of any organization. The efficiency with which a business uses these resources strongly influences how reliably it can grow and the duration of any success it may enjoy.

In nature, repeatability shows up in cycles and patterns (organizational models) that constantly renew themselves. Whether we examine the water cycle or the reproductive cycles of living organisms, repeatability is an essential component of a healthy system. In business, repeatability appears in the form of organizational models (processes, standards and systems) that offer predictable results. Scaling a business is difficult, but nearly impossible to accomplish if processes and systems are not repeatable.

As in nature, the business climate is always affected by change. Whether it be a drought or a torrential downpour, change is always influencing the repeatability and efficiency of natural ecosystems. And while individual influences may be hard to predict, one thing is for certain – change is always around the corner. In business, the ability to handle a diverse set of conditions is an excellent indicator of how strong a business model is. In the same way that forest fires create an environment for renewal of natural sub-ecosystems, a recession creates opportunity for businesses whose models gracefully accommodate change.

Without efficiency, systems fall out of balance and exhaust resources. Without repeatability, systems stagnate and fall into dysfunction and decline. Without resilience, systems are subject to a broader set of influences that can throw everything out of balance. Good business models are efficient, repeatable, and resilient systems.

■ ■ ■

Sam realizes that his company is not operating in an efficient or repeatable manner. Each PoC is customized and a lack of focus in marketing has them working on models for industries and company sizes that are far too diverse for any level of reasonable efficiency.

Regardless of how Stephen decides to account for the cost of PoCs, just executing each of these customized efforts in a repeatable and efficient manner is nearly impossible. They have allowed one of their strengths –the flexibility of their modeling software– to become a liability. What they are currently doing is the complete antithesis of a successful business model.

> *Is your business model efficient, repeatable and resilient?*

Feeling a bit overwhelmed, Sam forces himself to take a step back and evaluate the situation from a different perspective. Using a technique he remembers from business school, Sam decides to take an inventory of the organization's strengths and weaknesses.

| Strengths | Weaknesses |
|---|---|
| • The product is impressive and flexible. | • They are marketing to everyone– no focus. |
| • The product technically scales well. | • Custom PoCs are powerful but slow and costly to develop. |
| • They are well-funded by a strong VC firm. | • PoCs turn into custom solutions that require professional services. |
| • Their experienced CFO has done many IPOs and the company is positioned well for an exit. | • The more customized a solution becomes, the more complex pricing and contracts become. |
| • Everyone in the company stands to make a fortune if the company can execute their IPO before the favorable business climate sours. | • Pricing concessions are made because negotiations happen before the PoC demonstrates value. |
| • The value of their product becomes greater in bad economies when companies need to optimize their efficiencies. This factor makes the product very resilient. | • In good economies their customers don't require the optimized results that their product delivers so well. This tends to diminish their value proposition to prospective buyers. |

If they can focus their marketing efforts on a narrower set of industries and business cases, they can develop some repeatable PoCs that will not require customization for each client. Furthermore, if they can develop some "canned" models for specific industry problems, Sam believes the need for professional services can be significantly reduced. In turn, this should help standardize pricing and contractual processes that have been bogging down their sales velocity.

It's not that their product can't be used for all the customized scenarios they are working on today; it's that *now* is not the time to showcase the breadth of their product's capabilities. They will get more benefit by showing the depth of capability within a smaller set of focused industry problems. They must be able to demonstrate tangible customer value before pricing negotiations take place. They need a sales process that is more efficient and repeatable.

Even though Sam was not hired to re-tool the company's business model, he believes that a change in business model is the only way for his company to thrive. A new business model must improve the efficiency and repeatability they are currently lacking.

Sam knows that timing is critical. The economy is booming and his sales aren't. Sam must figure out how to sell more of his product faster or he is in big trouble.

He also knows that the IPO exit that is being planned for the organization is waiting on his ability to turn around the sales organization. The IPO is very important to the venture capital firm as well as his CFO. Furthermore, the success of their IPO will also hinge upon the economic environment when they go public. Now is the right time to take a company public, but that may not last... and Sam is not ready yet.

The clock is ticking and Sam needs to deliver his sales turnaround before the board gets impatient with him. His most urgent priority is to figure out who to work with to reshape the business model.

> *Who would you turn to if you were faced*
> *with a big problem like this?*

# 25

## STRATEGY

Strategy is not a bold prediction of the future nor is it the description of some idealized outcome. Implementing a strategy or running a business based on predictions of the future is akin to buying a lottery ticket to plan for retirement.

Good strategy requires an understanding of dependencies and possible outcomes. It is the study of variability and probability combined with the reality of what can be done at any given time. Strategy is not an abstract construct for academics; strategy is the cold hard truth of getting things done.

What makes strategy such a difficult concept for many is that successful strategies need to be both consistent and fluid at the same time. To be effective, strategies must be able to evolve with the changing conditions of the moment. And to be powerful, a strategy must always remain consistent with the overarching vision and values that define the soul of an organization. This juxtaposition of firmness and flexibility often prove difficult for people to comprehend and even more challenging for leaders to explain.

Successful strategies also require several disciplines that work against some of our most powerful impulses. Patience, timing, and sequencing are all disciplines that factor into winning strategies. All three work against our desire for immediate gratification and our natural bias toward action.

Patience has long been regarded as a virtue in Western philosophy or as a "perfection" in Eastern philosophies. In either case, patience has been held as an esteemed value for many centuries. Successful strategies require patience because results take time; and lasting results take even more time. Without patience, it is nearly impossible to achieve anything more than our most simplistic goals.

Steven Covey's famous quote *"begin with the end in mind"* is a wonderful way to capture the essence of sequencing. Strategy always starts with small beginnings. In chess, your strategy starts with the pawns. The first, and seemingly least important moves, often pave the way for success. Understanding the impact of each move is essential for a well-constructed strategy. Sequencing is the art of the next move and how each decision impacts your future options.

As John F. Kennedy said, *"The time to repair the roof is when the sun is shining."* Good timing is about recognizing conditions and avoiding problems as much as it is about seizing opportunity when it presents itself. But great timing is something special. Great timing generates results that have a disproportionate impact. Great timing is the art of knowing when a particular action will produce maximum impact.

All three of these disciplines –timing, sequencing, and patience– depend on one another. When you step back and examine them, it might be because they correlate nicely to the three ways in which we frame time– past, present, and future. Occasionally, we need to be patient, allowing precious time to pass us by. When we do act, good timing allows us to be the most efficient and effective in the moment. And our next best move is always informed by the context afforded by proper sequencing. Time is, and always will be, the thief that is never caught. Good strategy helps us extract the most out of the little time we are afforded.

■ ■ ■

Sam knows sales, but he has never been a C-level executive. He finds the situation he is in a bit awkward. Sam is certain that the business model is not where it needs to be for him to address the sales gap that currently exists, but he is unsure of where to start. Taking a cue from Socrates, Sam accepts that there is much about the company that he does not yet know. With that in mind, Sam schedules time with his CEO.

The CEO is an amazing person and the brilliant mind that founded the company. He is only 34 years old and holds just as many patents. He is a bona fide genius. Sam sits with the CEO for over three hours and learns about the company history as well as his vision for the product. In a nutshell, the CEO hopes that their product will help model and solve the greatest problems we face as a human race. His goal is to be the engine that helps cure cancer, eliminate hunger, and solve crimes. It is exciting and inspirational to spend time with him and it is no wonder he has attracted so many high-profile investors to support the development of their product.

For as much as Sam is impressed by his founder's intellect and passion, he is left wanting more substance on the near-term milestones that need to take place before they start curing cancer. Although he asks many probing questions, Sam never receives the clarity he seeks. Every answer, however eloquent, is always focused on the bright future his CEO someday hopes to unlock. Sam knows one thing for sure –hope is not a winning strategy.

Sam is left wondering. What is his company's overall strategy? His CEO has described a brilliant future, but no path to get there. His CFO has an exit strategy, but how does that help the company the day after it goes public?

A great strategy never focuses on an outcome alone. It's the same reason a military strategy sounds foolish if we just say– *win the battle*. A strategy will include a plan on how to win the battle as well as a description of the conditions we would expect after victory is achieved. The problem for Sam is… whose definition of victory guides their strategy?

> ***What does victory look like for you?***
> ***Does your strategy provide a path to get there?***

# 26

## LEADERSHIP

Few topics have been studied throughout history more than leadership. And even with all that attention, leadership is still hard to define, describe, and teach. There are as many definitions of leadership as there are stars in the sky.

Leadership cannot be encapsulated in a singular moment, a courageous deed, or a bold statement– it is the culmination of many small actions that often go unnoticed. Leadership is about maintaining the delicate balance that is necessary for groups of people to work together productively.

- Good leadership makes sure people are busy, but not too busy.
- Good leadership fosters healthy conflicts and debate but keeps that conflict from becoming personal and detrimental.
- Good leadership holds people accountable, but still allows them to make mistakes, grow and learn.
- Good leadership fosters strong cultures and consistent values without sacrificing openness to new people and ideas.
- Good leadership helps individuals become the best versions of themselves while helping teams do more than any individual could ever accomplish on their own.
- Good leadership is benevolent, fair, and balanced.

But good leadership is always in short supply. Perhaps this is because balance is exceptionally difficult to establish and maintain. Maybe this is because balance can be in conflict with maximized outcomes. Or perhaps this is because balance frequently requires compromise. Perhaps this is because leadership touches every aspect of how we interact.

Accordingly, one could argue that all problems eventually come down to failures in leadership. The old saying that *"a fish rots from the head"* does suggest that all problems start at the top. As appealing as it is to find a singular source for all our problems, that temptation must be resisted. Once we abdicate our personal responsibility to the poor leadership of others, we surrender any notion of liberty and autonomy.

Leadership is about acknowledging what we can't control and doing the best we can with what we can control. Leadership is knowing which problems to ignore and which problems to solve. Leadership is not about authority and hierarchy; leadership is all about the individual responsibility we have for our own actions and those we can influence, including who we choose to follow.

We are at our best in business and in life when we refuse to be subjugated by rigid hierarchies and dogmas. Our curiosity, creativity and our virtue are always within our control. Albert Einstein wisely stated that *"we cannot solve our problems with the same level of thinking that created them."* And that is exactly why a fish does not have to rot from the head.

■ ■ ■

Sam's three-hour meeting with their founder confirmed the visionary genius that has attracted so much interest from investors and prospects. But the details behind the execution of any strategy are scant. Aside from a technology roadmap, Sam did not get a comprehensive vision of how all the pieces fit together.

Sam spends the next week speaking with nearly every executive within the company. When it is all said and done, he is no further than when he started. His CEO's technology strategy and product roadmap are phenomenal. The IPO exit strategy driven by the CFO is pragmatic and sound. The marketing lead generation strategy is producing a steady stream of customer interest. Every leader he speaks with has a plan for their group, but nobody seems to have an overall vision. Everything but the go-to-market strategy –Sam's biggest concern– seems to be addressed.

This whole situation strikes Sam as very odd. It's as if his company is an all-star team packed with talent, without a coach to guide them. A coach surely would have noticed the absence of a go-to-market strategy.

At this point, Sam is starting to get upset with himself. How did he let his enthusiasm and excitement blind him from such obvious flaws with his new company? What had he just done? Not only had Sam left a lucrative position, but he has also invested his family's future into this firm. How can he possibly face his wife, Sarah?

Sam now realizes that he will need to create the go-to-market strategy on his own. He accepts that responsibility, but he is still troubled. The issue gnawing at Sam is that there does not seem to be a holistic business strategy for the company. In fact, Sam doesn't even know who, if anyone, is leading that effort. Moreover, he is disturbed by the accelerated push toward an IPO. Sam knows that this will be a huge financial windfall for many of the investors, but it just doesn't feel right.

Sam wonders about what will happen to the company once all of the investors cash-out. Even more troubling is the thought of who will no longer care about the company after the IPO. Will his brilliant CEO be left alone at the helm? Will the cancer curing promise of this company ever be realized?

*Have you ever felt the despair of a decision you realize you did not think through sufficiently?*

# 27

## SAM'S RISKY PROPOSITION

For the first several years, the company worked at perfecting their technology. And to that end they have been quite successful. Everything is running efficiently and producing outstanding results for their customers. The exit strategy for this business is through an Initial Public Offering (IPO); an execution plan that Stephen knows exceptionally well. The only thing holding up the timing of the IPO is the creation of a wave of momentum through a strong and growing sales pipeline. And that is exactly why Sam is the new VP of sales, and the focus of the next board meeting.

Everyone thinks the last lingering issue to be tackled with the company is sales. Sam disagrees. Sales is clearly an issue, but it is not the core problem they are facing. Sam does not believe that their business model is sustainable. They can surely get to an IPO, but the promise of this company and its revolutionary technology will never be realized. Sam fears that investors in the IPO will be buying into an empty promise.

Through his research, Sam has discovered that there are many dependencies and problems involved here. The key is to identify the problem that needs to be solved first and then develop the sequence of changes that will eventually allow them to boost sales.

Sam believes that the core problem is a lack of focus. Right now, they need to focus on high-value situations that can be sold quickly. They need a strategy whereby they establish a foothold, gain momentum, and eventually parlay that momentum to other problems. Casting a wide net has cost them dearly.

A greater focus on targeted industry problems will allow them to develop "canned" models that demonstrate tangible value. This will eliminate the need for costly customized PoCs and establish a business model that can grow and scale profitably. The business model change will also facilitate shorter sales cycles and the sales velocity that he was hired to deliver. If they can be a bit patient with sales and focus their efforts on the core problem, Sam is confident he can fulfill the expectations for him as the new leader of the sales organization.

And while that may be the problem for the company, the problem for Sam is that what he is proposing is dramatically different from the do-everything-for-everyone vision of their brilliant founder. Furthermore, he is the new sales leader who has yet to increase the company's sales. How can the new guy raise this issue when it looks like it could be an excuse for poor performance?

Sam is terrified. He has invested so much into this company that a failure here could be devastating to him and his family. He knows he needs to speak up, but he also fears it could cost him his job. In fact, the very VCs that brought him in might be anxious to usher him out as fast as they discarded his predecessor.

On top of all this is the fear that his wife Sarah was right. Perhaps he should have been more conservative with their personal investments into this company. Or perhaps they should have been satisfied with what the company had originally given them. Sam is scared to even speak with Sarah about his concerns.

Regardless, Sam knows that Sarah suspects he is concerned about work. Sleepless nights and early morning workouts are dead giveaways that signal when Sam is stressed out.

That evening, Sam confides his findings and fears with Sarah. The two have a heartfelt conversation wherein Sarah supports him to do the right thing. Sam adores his wife and knows she is clearly the better half of their relationship. He confides that he doesn't know how to articulate the problem the company is having without making it sound like an excuse for his inability to quickly turn around sales. Sarah lets him know that she is confident he will figure it out, just as he has always done in the past.

Sam understands that he can't call out the company's strategy or business model as bad. He's pretty sure that will get him escorted out of the building. What he believes he can do, however, is to suggest there is a factor that was overlooked in the business model. If he can add this new factor into the discussion, perhaps, he can gently guide the company into a new direction.

But Sam also has to muster up the courage to communicate his point. He knows that courage is not simply saying something shocking. The kind of courage that is useful in the workplace is about responsibly preparing a challenging message so that it can be received well. Sam isn't trying to make a point; he needs to make change.

Sam wrestles with his challenging communication dilemma for nearly a week. His first board meeting is in a few days, and he is still trying to figure out the best way to guide the company strategy in a more productive direction. Sam has attended board meetings in the past, but he has never been in the hot seat like this.

While he is finally clear on the sequence of events needed to address his sales problem, Sam is still unclear on how to get everyone else on board with his idea. The concepts are plain to see, but the trick is how to navigate the politics and the emotional invest-ment so many people have with their current business practices. Sam is exhausted thinking through all the complexities and politics involved. Reaching the end of his rope, Sam relents and considers the fact that he might need some help.

Sam considers a risky option. His gut instinct with his sales leadership team is that they are good people that care about the company, their team, and their customers. He is going to share his findings with his leaders and see if they have any suggestions on how to "sell" the board. The risk is that any one of them could back-channel his ideas to the board, subvert his efforts, and posi-tion themselves for his job. But with confidence in his instincts and virtuous intent on his side, Sam believes the risk is worth it.

Sam gathers his team and shares his insights. His team is excited and relieved. They are relieved in the sense that there is now a plan, and they are excited to finally have a sales leader that is listening to them and their customers. The strategy Sam describes seems to mirror many of their concerns and suggestions of the past several years. Their prior leader, as Sam now learns, was not too keen on wanting or listening to their feedback. Sam's gamble seems to be paying off.

After several hours of liberating conversation with his team, Sam walks away with two wonderful suggestions. The first sugges-tion is that he focuses all his energy communicating in the context of time. Time is what the board cares about most. The second sug-gestion comes from a phrase that was uttered casually by one of his leaders. His leader spoke about the friction he feels externally with customer adoption and internally with the complicated PoCs. If they could just get rid of that friction, everything would move faster. Sam loves that word and knows exactly how he will use it in his presentation.

As he concludes the meeting, he is careful not to ask for their discretion on this matter. If someone is going to the board behind his back, they would do so regardless of what he says. He knows that trust is not a quid-pro-quo agreement; trust is something you earn. He then closes with this statement:

*"Thank you for your extremely valuable input. I know you have been let down in the past, but I promise I will not let you down. You can trust me to advocate for this plan, for our customers and for you. I'm confident your suggestions will be a critical part of our mutual success."*

In the back of Sam's mind, he thinks to himself— *I hope I can finally sleep well tonight… It's been too long.*

The day has finally arrived— Sam's first board meeting. A few months ago, Sam imagined this very day with a room full of board members amazed at the turnaround he had just completed. On this morning, however, Sam knows the reception of his message will not be the triumphant victory he had once imagined.

After a few opening remarks and procedural board issues, Sales is the primary topic on the agenda. The board is eager to hear what their new hire has done in the months since he joined the company. Sam feels as though he is under a magnifying glass. And he is.

In his heart, Sam knows he must come clean about his findings without sounding like he is coming up with excuses.

In a very subtle and clever manner, Sam suggests that the product is so advanced and exceptionally powerful that the value can be difficult for their customers to comprehend. He is quick to praise the professional services team for the wonderful PoCs they create to help put their solution into customer-centric contexts.

Sam carefully avoids talking about the cost of the PoCs, but he does mention the time they take to develop. Sam also stays away from the pricing issues that are driven by contracts that are negotiated before value is demonstrated. Sam knows that the key issue for his board members is time– speeding up the sales process to enable an IPO. All his comments will focus on the one thing that matters: time.

Sam then introduces the notion that they need to get more use out of each PoC to speed up the process. The time to develop each PoC introduces a level of friction into the sales cycle. If they can eliminate that "sales friction", the whole process will move faster.

Sam suggests that if they focus on a few specific industries with pre-built –or "canned"– models, they can speed up the sales process tremendously.

As soon as Sam is done speaking there is dead silence. The board members and his other colleagues appear shocked by the direction Sam has taken with his first board appearance. An awkward mood permeates the room and lingers in the stunned silence. But Sam is smart enough to let the silence continue. It is not his place to speak. Doubling down on his argument now only makes his position weaker. He has said what needed to be said.

Some board members are clearly perturbed by Sam's comments. It is also clear that others are waiting for someone else to speak up. Sam makes eye contact with several board members and observes a stare that he imagines might have approximated what Julius Caesar saw moments before daggers were drawn on him.

Regardless, Sam is at peace with what he has just said. In the same vein, he knows all too well that this could be his very first and last board meeting for this company.

The awkward and painful silence is finally broken by a board observer who also happens to be the single largest individual investor in the company. This investor is a notable and experienced entrepreneur named Simon who has had many successful exits with technology companies. When Simon speaks, people listen:

*"If our goal here is to make money for the shareholders represented today… Sam's comments and insights will most certainly delay our plans. If our goal is to create a company that makes money for current and future shareholders, Sam is 100% correct. I've been running the numbers and Sam's strategy creates a much stronger SaaS business model. I know I'm not a voting board member, but I will voice my opinion that this company has been on the wrong track. Sam's strategy is as brilliant as the technology behind this company. I know that the institutional money represented on the board is obligated to act in the best interest of their investor base. However, as respectable business people and citizens, we owe it to future shareholders to provide a company that is positioned for success. How can we possibly proceed with an IPO for a company with a flawed business model? Where is our virtue?"*

Sam takes his first breath in what seems like ten minutes. Simon's comments and support alleviate a pressure upon his shoulders that felt like the weight of the world. Simon casts a glance of respect to Sam that means more to him than anything at this moment. Sam gently nods back with an immeasurable level of gratitude.

At this point, you would think that all attention would point back to the CEO, or at least the Chairman of the Board, for a response. Strangely, though, all eyes go straight to Stephen –the CFO.

It's now abundantly clear that Stephen is the keeper of the business strategy. The plan was an IPO… and everyone just had to play their role for the plan to work. Whatever is said next shall be a moment of truth for Sam, for Stephen, and for the entire organization.

Stephen takes a moment to gather his thoughts and the pregnant pause in his response is palpable. When he finally speaks, it is not a declarative statement or the "dagger" that Sam feared. Stephen poses a simple question to Sam:

*"How long do you think it would take to re-tool our business model to focus on fewer industries with less customized or more pre-built solutions?"*

Sam is shocked by Stephen's question. In fact, it is one of the few responses he had not prepared for. Like a true professional, however, Sam quickly gathers his thoughts and responds.

*"Six months,"* are the words that confidently stream from Sam's mouth.

Stephen then responds with another question, *"Will we have more sales in six months or are you telling us that we will just be ready to sell our simplified solutions in six months?"*

It is another great question that Sam had not considered. Sam thinks aloud as he explains his rationale: *"If we can identify a suitable industry problem within one month, we should be able to build a model in the following month. We just have to make sure that the problem is widespread enough to provide sufficient market opportunity. In the month thereafter we should be able to pilot it with at least one company to demonstrate positive results. Marketing can then start targeting companies that fit our new "canned" model profile. If we can keep to that timetable, we will have three months for the sales team to prove out a faster sales process with far less friction. It's tight, but I think we can show significant growth in our sales velocity by the end of six months. We should be able to double the number of closed monthly deals and our pipeline will be stronger."*

Stephen quickly responds, *"Great, that is still within the projected window for a favorable IPO and the stronger pipeline should boost our public offering price. If we can meet those timelines everything can still proceed as planned. Of course, I motion that we accelerate the pace of board meetings to assess our progress."*

Without hesitation, the Chairman of the Board –who represents the lead venture capitalist firm– asks for and receives a second on the motion to accelerate the pace of board meetings.

Going into the board meeting, Sam was terrified of what could go wrong. But he stuck to his principles and made a strong case that –to his surprise– was received well. And while he feels a sense of vindication from Simon's support and a sense of relief from the six-month reprieve… the pressure of his situation has increased tenfold. The clock is ticking and Sam has six months to prove his point and make a difference.

Naturally, as soon as the meeting ends Sam calls his wife Sarah. She was anxious to know the outcome of the board meeting. They are both relieved that his message was received well and that he still has his job.

Later that evening, Sam confides with Sarah the immense pressure he now feels to deliver on his plan. Sarah hugs her husband and pecks him on the cheek. She expresses how proud she is of him. He had the courage to do what was right. He had the curiosity to dig into the real problem instead of accepting what was handed to him. Furthermore, he had the creativity to find a solution and sell it properly to the board.

That is why he was able to see the problem for what it was. That is why he was able to see a clear path forward. The remaining path will not be easy, but she comforts Sam by letting him know the toughest part of the job –finding the core problem– is already in the rear-view mirror.

# PART III

## A CURIOUS POWER

I was fortunate to be exposed to computer programming in the 1970's through my childhood friend, Mark. His father had dial-up access to a mainframe via a teletype machine and a phone coupler–very old school. We played a game called "Colossal Cave" for hours on end. We also dabbled a bit in programming before the personal computer even existed. Computing and programming were fantastic playgrounds for curious minds.

After my first programming class in college, my interest in computers took a nosedive. I no longer understood them and they no longer liked me or my GPA. I remember telling my fraternity brother John that I NEVER wanted to do anything with computers for the rest of my life.

I developed a scheme to get through the programming requirements for my major. Without this ingenious plan, a passing grade was questionable. The scheme involved me getting to the computer lab as soon as it opened on the day assignments were due. At that time, you turned in a physical printout of your work on large format green bar computer paper. Success depended on getting a seat right near the large garbage cans that people threw their printouts into. If you paid attention to the smarter programmers who were trying to ace the assignment, the frequency of their trips to the garbage bin would increase as they got closer to the "perfect" printout. By pulling printouts from the garbage, I was able to see how they thought and how they progressively addressed challenges. I envied how they framed the problems and the creative methods they used to solve them. None of this came naturally to me.

Make no mistake, though, I would have likely spent another semester in college if it were not for this unconventional approach. I may not have learned to program, but I learned something much more important. The skill I developed in college was how to spot and build relationships with top talent. I learned early how to spot the smart engineers. They were the ones to know. They were the ones who knew so much that they got excited to share everything they knew. They were good friends and wonderful lab partners!

This undocumented "engineering management degree" served me well in my professional career. A perfect example of this was a programmer by the name of Ken Fox.

Ken and I worked together and became friendly. He was a brilliant programmer who was way ahead of his time. At one point he was sent to California for some technology transfer with a defense industry component of our parent company. Upon his return, he was eager to share what he saw. Ken invited me down to his dark basement office with his typical geeky excitement. He said, *"You are not going to believe this. I'm going to show you something so cool."*

Ken then proceeded to show me a green screen of random characters that looked like something straight out of the Matrix movies (Wachowski, 1999). He said, *"That's a picture of a guy with his dog and a frisbee and the dog has a handkerchief around his neck. He's in California and he just sent this to me via this network called the World Wide Web and it's going to be everywhere."* I wasn't impressed and I certainly didn't see the value. It still looked like a bunch of random characters.

Several months later he tricked me into coming to his office by telling me he had something new and cool that was from my alma mater, the University of Illinois. He showed me the same picture of the dog with the handkerchief around his neck. This time I could see it in vivid color. The picture was rendered through the Graphics Interchange Format (GIF) via an early beta copy of Mosaic, one of the very first web browsers.

It was sooooo cool! It also had words on the page. They were formatted and some of them were even blinking. Not only that, but a few words were also underlined in bright blue. When you clicked on them it took you somewhere else. It was amazing.

I told Ken, *"Now this is cool. That other thing you showed me was junk."* Ken, laughing at my ignorance, let me know that it was the same thing. The browser was just a new way to experience the World Wide Web.

I still have clear memories of that conversation. I knew it was important. This was a big deal. I was curious and I wanted to learn more. I needed to know how it worked and how I could create web pages of my very own.

As it turns out, that was a seminal moment in my professional career. The programming skill I once lacked was now something I sought. The frustrations I once had were challenges I welcomed. Now that I had a clear vision of the future, my fears abated and my talents could be focused on a new horizon.

Over time, I began to realize the common theme between my college frustrations and my newfound passion was curiosity. In college, I was curious about the people behind the magic. After Ken showed me the World Wide Web, my curiosity shifted to the actual magic.

I often wondered why it took me so long to see things. Perhaps I was of a lesser intellect. Based on my college performance, that was a strong possibility. Later in my career, I realized that *context* is what turned on the light bulb for me. The random characters Ken initially showed me lacked context, but the picture was rich with context. The homework assignments in college had no purpose or context for me– the Internet did.

The remainder of this section will focus on the importance both curiosity and context play in developing a clear picture of the past, present, or future.

# 28

## CASE STUDY – GEORGE

George is the general manager and vice president of operations for a manufacturer of assemblies and gears used in light-industrial truck transmissions. The company has been based in the same midwestern city for over 100 years and is an important part of the community. Approximately ten years ago, the privately held manufacturing icon was purchased by a large publicly traded corporation.

While many lamented the purchase of the company by the manufacturing conglomerate, history has shown it to be a wonderful acquisition. Large capital investments by the parent company allowed for huge gains in productivity and competitive positioning. Additionally, the overall reach and influence of the conglomerate facilitated partnerships that have fueled tremendous growth.

George is the third generation of his family to make a career out of working for this company. He never imagined that he would be the top executive running this manufacturing plant when he was working in the factory during high school. In many ways, this company has been an integral part of his family for as long as he can remember.

The gears that George's company makes have been in high demand for many years. As the automotive market moved to SUV's, light-trucks, and all-wheel drivetrains, the need for their specialty gears has grown dramatically. This very favorable confluence of events has made it quite fun to lead Operations for this division. With the help of their parent company, George has been able to fund dramatic capital investments in machinery and automation to expand their market leadership position.

For as well as things have been going, George is concerned about his company's future. Electric cars have been slowly eroding the business of gear manufacturers that serve lower-end automotive applications. The gears for transmissions and other key linkages are largely unnecessary with electric vehicles. Many people, including George's parent company, think that the higher end of the light-industrial market will be spared as more demanding applications will stick with conventional combustion engines and drivetrains. Based on his own instincts, George is wary of this overconfidence.

George and his division have been the darling of his parent company with quarterly results that have supported steady growth. However, the continuous pressure to deliver financial performance weighs heavy on George. Rumors are circulating that key customers will soon announce plans for electric vehicle options on various truck models that are close to the bread-and-butter categories for his division.

George is unwilling to let the future of his division, the welfare of his employees, and the prosperity of his hometown depend on a belief that his customers will reject electrified vehicles. Furthermore, George understands that small decreases in volume will have disproportionate effects on profitability due to the high depreciation costs from the many capital investments he has implemented.

The stakes are very high and George doesn't know anything about electric cars. George knows that the answers he needs lie in information he does not yet have.

> *What do you care about enough to challenge the status quo and ask uncomfortable questions?*

# 29

## CONTEXT IS KING

Whether your circumstances are simple or complicated, context is one of the most determinant factors in achieving clarity with your thinking. The clear path forward is always influenced by how you frame a problem, the constraints of the situation, and the many possible perspectives taken by individual stakeholders. Moreover, the urgency of a situation always plays a crucial role in limiting what can realistically be evaluated before decisions need to be made. The context of any situation influences your ability to accurately assess a situation as well as the available options.

Consider two gourmet burger restaurants located across the street from one another. One restaurant –John's– is a well-known establishment that has won awards and has been featured on popular television programs. They advertise locally and their active social media presence frequently touts the long lines of patrons waiting to experience their tasty burgers. The other restaurant –Mary's– is lesser known and barely advertises. Even though Mary's burgers are just as good as their competitor, there are never lines of people waiting outside.

Which restaurant is more successful?

By all accounts, most people would conclude that John's gourmet burger joint is more successful. John's is well-known, it has won awards, it has been featured on television and there is always a line outside. In contrast, Mary's has none of these things.

But it is possible that we are missing valuable context that might alter our perceptions? Fortunately, without the pressure of urgency, we are afforded the time to seek additional information to help us evaluate the situation.

Let's see how the context changes dramatically with one question. *Are the restaurants at full capacity?*

If we find out that both restaurants are at full capacity, we might scratch our heads in disbelief. But as it turns out, Mary's is the benefactor of the long lines at John's. Mary's enjoys a steady stream of hungry customers eager to enjoy a gourmet burger without the wait. In fact, Mary's puts through 20% more customers per hour because they have more seating than John's. On top of that, the customers at Mary's frequently order highly profitable appetizers because they are famished after abandoning the long wait at John's.

We might now conclude that Mary's is the more successful restaurant. With 20% higher throughput and minimal marketing costs, Mary's must be more profitable. But we have yet to consider so many other important factors that may provide additional context. *Are their prices the same? Are their costs the same? Furthermore, how are we defining success?*

If their prices and costs are similar, Mary's may very well be more profitable. And if profitability is our measure of success– Mary's wins. But if our measure of success is linked to the popularity and broad appeal that may help John's set the stage for franchising; perhaps John's is set up to be more successful.

The void created by questions unasked is filled with assumptions that comfort our sensibilities but dull our intellect. Our assumptions limit our ability to see different perspectives and consider more challenging questions. And those same challenging questions are the ones that can most alter our perspective.

Now consider this situation: You have just finished a wonderful dinner on a beautiful summer evening. You find yourself walking through the entrance of a fancy casino feeling like a million bucks. In front of you is the roulette wheel, several blackjack tables and a dozen craps tables. Surrounding them all is a sea of slot and video poker machines. *Which game has the best odds?*

There are vast and complicated arguments on whether roulette or craps or blackjack have the best odds. So, what is the key question to ask to determine which game has the best odds? What is the house advantage? What are the payout amounts? Those are fine questions. But perhaps the most important question is this: *Who am I?*

What if you were not a player at the casino, but the owner of that very casino you walked into? How would that change your perspective? The original question quickly becomes much easier. Your sea of slot machines makes you money almost every time those wheels start spinning. The math can be simple when you clearly understand your perspective.

There is always more information to seek and another question to ask, that is the trouble with context. At some point, though, enough is enough. The key is to ask the most revealing questions as early as possible. This skill not only helps in urgent situations, but it also reduces the overall mental burden of every situation. And the only way to get better at finding the perfect question quickly is to develop the habit of always asking questions. Practice. Practice. Practice.

Nowhere is this better demonstrated than with entrepreneurs. People often view entrepreneurs as bigger risk takers or even gamblers. This is a very narrow and uninformed perspective. Unsuccessful entrepreneurs might be bigger risk takers, but successful serial entrepreneurs are not. The successful entrepreneurs, of which I've known many, are far superior at evaluating risk. In fact, many of the most successful entrepreneurs and investors I know have lower risk tolerances than the average businessperson.

What makes them different is that they are curious and demanding. They aggressively seek the additional context that surrounds any situation or opportunity. They seek to understand. For them, the risks are lower. They may appear to be bigger risk takers, but that is from the perspective of someone who has not done the work to understand the full context of a situation.

■ ■ ■

Near the end of every quarter, the pressure on George hits a peak. Once he submits his numbers and the parent company issues their quarterly report, he can finally relax. If the results are good, George always tries to get away to unwind with his family.

This quarter he escapes to the coast twelve hours away. Most executives would fly, but George has always preferred the calming effect of a long drive. His wife Grace tolerates these road trips because she knows that her husband will unwind and de-stress as he drives through the mountains and down to the coast.

George has four children that love the beach and playing in the ocean surf. Grace loves the warm sun and the peaceful sound of the waves steadily rolling into the shore. George just likes seeing his family happy. By all accounts, George is living the dream.

Even on vacations, George usually rises before his family and goes out for a short walk to get his morning coffee. The early morning peace and quiet is a great way to relax before his lively crew starts their day. George quietly enjoys a cup of coffee on the boardwalk patio as he reads his paper copy of the Wall Street Journal. It is part of a morning routine he likes to continue even when he is on vacation.

This morning, an interesting article on electric bikes sparks his interest. George doesn't see many electric bikes back in his hometown, but they are everywhere here by the ocean. With his curiosity fully piqued, George walks a bit further down the boardwalk to a shop that rents bikes to tourists.

George engages the clerk in a discussion about electric bikes. George asks why they are so popular and how they are different from normal bikes. Aside from the fact that the electric bikes make pedaling far easier —especially going uphill— there are fewer differences than he would have expected. To George, the electric bikes seem like quite an interesting innovation.

Still curious, George asks about the two types of electric bikes he sees in the shop. Some have normal sized tires and others have big fat tires. The clerk explains how the bikes with narrow tires are great for riding around town and how the fat tire bikes are made for off-road trail riding.

George then asks if there are any other differences, besides the tires, that make the off-road bikes better. *"Indeed, there are,"* says the clerk as he engages George with more enthusiasm. *"The biggest difference is in the drive hub. The road bikes are direct drive, but the off-road bikes have a geared hub to provide more low-end torque. It makes all the difference in the world when you are on the trail."*

The two speak for a few more minutes as the clerk begins to talk about the bike he owns and why the brand he favors is better than another brand. It is a detailed discussion that quickly loses George's interest.

Looking at his watch, George thanks the clerk for his time and heads back to the beach house. If he doesn't get back soon to help Grace get the family ready for the beach, he will hear about it later. After all, this is her vacation too.

Following a few too many days in the sun and not enough aloe to comfort burnt shoulders, the family decides to take a break from the beach. George tries to get everyone interested in renting electric bikes, but that idea goes nowhere. Disappointed, but not discouraged, George arranges a fun day of 4x4 vehicle off-roading near some large rock formations and sand dunes an hour away. Grace is not thrilled with the choice, but the kids are excited and so is George.

The ex-military drivers took their modified Humvees over rocks and up hills that none of them thought they could climb. The rapid descents into deep sand pits were equally thrilling and unbelievable. Aside from a healthy coating of sand in every nook and cranny, everyone had a great time. The kids wanted more, but George could tell that Grace had reached her limit of off-road fun.

As George thanks his driver with a generous tip, he asks him all about his vehicle and some of the modifications they had made. He is curious to know what makes these seemingly impossible maneuvers so effortless. George is stunned to learn that there are strikingly few modifications to the stock military surplus vehicle. As he inspects further, he realizes that the vehicles' exceptional ground clearance is not achieved with the normal suspension technologies seen on the vehicles his company services. Instead, his driver informs him that the Humvee uses a long-abandoned suspension technology called a portal axle. Although highly effective, this technology is rarely used commercially because it is cost-prohibitive in most modern vehicles.

But before George can dig deeper, the kids end his geeky interlude with the military veteran to remind him that they are all hungry.

After a wonderful lunch, everyone falls asleep as George drives the family back to their beach house. Alone in his thoughts, George wonders if his company is making their own version of the portal axle– an effective technology that is about to be phased out of existence.

# 30

## PRESSURE TESTING ASSUMPTIONS

Many times, throughout my career I was a "fixer" for troubled projects and client relationships. It was a role I didn't seek, but others saw that I was good in that role. The funny part is that nobody quite knew why I was good in that role. In fact, it took me years to understand the source of my competence.

On the surface, I was successful because I could quickly build rapport and trust with all the involved parties. This is an incredibly important skill set. However, this skill set was not the key to my success and did not provide any context for how to avoid lurking problems.

My success was due to the fact that I could quickly identify the core problem behind the troubled project or client relationship. I didn't know why it came so easy to me, but time after time I was always able to accurately assess the situation.

Honestly, I didn't know the source of my competence. Was it luck? I possessed no greater mastery of the subject matter than those around me and, in many cases, far less experience. I worried that the lucky streak might run out and that I would be found out to be a fraud. What was the secret that led to so many successful outcomes?

I found the answer one day when I was using some twine to tie my trunk shut after a home improvement purchase for our new home. I had to search the far corners of my car for a suitable length of twine to secure the load for the ride home. Only one piece was long enough, but it was a bit frayed in one spot from a previous trip. As I tightened it down, it snapped... exactly where the twine was weakest.

It was no surprise. If a rope is going to break, it is going to break where it is frayed. In fact, anything that breaks always seems to break where it is weakest.

I realized the same may be true for the business situations I was asked to "fix." I figured that the secret to my success may lie in an ability to quickly identify the "frayed portion of the rope." In the next several client engagements, I paid close attention to the cues that were feeding my intuition. What was it that I was hearing that was providing me the insights that were clearly so valuable?

As it turns out, I was quick to identify when people were making assumptions. And like the frayed rope, problems usually occurred right where assumptions were being made.

Even with all the information in the world at our fingertips, it is impossible to know everything. Assumptions enable speed in a world with few spare cycles and a shortage of time. Assumptions are a shortcut - just like using the frayed rope one last time.

Not all assumptions are bad. In urgent situations, they can be useful shortcuts that save time and prevent problems from growing larger. We get into trouble, though, when our assumptions create unnecessary and unrecognized risks that make our problems larger.

When an assumption is made, it is important to understand exactly why this shortcut was necessary:

- Could this assumption be eliminated?
- Is there time to try and eliminate this assumption?

- Are there any facts supporting this assumption?
- Do any facts depend on this assumption being correct?
- What is the risk associated with this assumption?

In many cases, our assumptions seem to work in the short term. However, as time passes and conditions change, our assumptions reveal themselves– often in a destructive manner. This is where pressure testing your assumptions comes into play.

If we study fields that routinely plan for catastrophic outcomes, we can learn from their methods to improve processes more appropriate for broader business contexts.

Consider engineers building a bridge, water tower or pipeline. Before these items are built and made operational, they are tested in extreme conditions: hurricane force winds, earthquakes, as well as pressures and temperatures well above safety limits.

We can apply the same concept of pressure testing to ensure the validity of a strategy or plan. The key is to take any situation and stress it to ridiculous levels. Consider these examples:

- What happens if every deal in the pipeline closes?
- What if regulation makes our business untenable?
- What happens if all the pensioners live to be 120?

The key is not to ruminate on the likelihood of an unlikely scenario. The key is to see how the impact of an assumption is clarified by considering extreme circumstances.

Just as a pressurized vessel will burst at the site of a weak weld, a business plan or strategy will fail at the site of an assumption. The weak points in our logic and decisions are frequently rooted in the assumptions we make.

Clarifying assumptions can be an important way to reinforce thinking and strengthen any plan of action. Three simple steps are all that is necessary.

First, it is important to assess the reason why an assumption was made. Was it out of convenience? Experience? Urgency? Understanding the rationale behind an assumption is the first step toward clarifying its utility and purpose. The origin of an assumption is valuable context to evaluate the decision-making process. And assumptions typically highlight flaws in the decision-making process the same way poor welds reveal the weak points in a structure.

Next, it is useful to clarify the limits of an assumption. It is critical to know the endpoints of the range of any assumption. The safe operating margin of any assumption is the equivalent of the maximum operating temperature of a device or the maximum pressure a vessel can withstand. Understanding the working limits of any assumption provides the safe operating range within which an assumption remains valid.

Lastly, it is essential to eliminate the weak points in a decision-making process. Just as engineers strive to eliminate the weak points in any design, it is important to eliminate the weak points in any plan or strategy. This does not mean that all points of failure must be eliminated, but it does mean that the most likely sources of failure should be mitigated. In a business plan or strategy, this would be the assumptions whose endpoints fall within the expected operating limits of the business. Many of these assumptions can be eliminated with fact-based research and constructive dialogue with colleagues. Gathering different perspectives is the hard work that reinforces thinking to help any decision-making process hold up under strain.

Practitioners that pressure test their assumptions and strengthen the weak points in their logic tend to produce business strategies and plans that are stronger, more capable, and yield more consistent results.

■ ■ ■

The vacation is over, and the ride home has just started. In typical fashion, George is the only one awake in the car. But that doesn't bother him. George enjoys driving on the open road. There is something liberating about highway driving that has always relaxed him.

As he is driving George is starting to notice more and more electric vehicles. He isn't sure if there are actually more electric cars on the road or if it is because he has been thinking about them lately. Regardless, George knows he needs to learn more about this shift in the automotive marketplace.

With about four hours under his belt and far too much coffee, George starts to look for a suitable exit. Eventually, a good exit with plenty of options for gas and food catches his interest. As he heads off the highway and onto the exit ramp, he notices three electric vehicles exiting with him. George wonders why there is such a concentration of electric cars getting off the highway at this particular exit. Is there something special about this exit or is he just hypersensitive to electric vehicles now that he is thinking about them more?

With his curiosity engaged and his family still asleep, George decides to follow the electric cars. The small parade of electric cars passes by all the convenient gas stations that line the side of the road near the exit. After driving a few miles further, the cars pull into an expansive gas station in the parking lot of a large chain store. There are many gas pumps and what looks like six electric charging stations. George picks the gas pump nearest to the electric charging stations.

As he fills up his car, he strikes up a conversation with the owner of the car next to him. George starts the conversation simply: *"How do you like your electric car?"*

That's all George needed to say. The owner of the car goes into a full-on sales pitch on the awesomeness of electric vehicles. Aside from the typical fuel economy boost and the many environmental benefits, a few points stand out for George:

- The cars are very reliable. They have far fewer moving parts and linkages and they never need oil changes.
- The absence of the traditional transmission makes the inside of the vehicle much more open and luxurious.
- They are amazingly fast, responsive, and fun to drive.
- The self-driving features and frequent software updates constantly improve the driving experience.
- Charging stations are far and few between so that is a bit of a problem until more charging stations are built.
- Long road trips are tougher because you are forced to plan your route around the location of charging stations.
- Electric vehicles generally sit low to the ground, so potholes and road debris are a bigger concern than they are for big SUVs like George's car.

By now, George's family is up and out of the car, making their trips to the restroom and grabbing snacks from the mini mart. Familiar with the routine, Grace is already back at the car with a fresh cup of coffee for George. She gently reminds him that his pump had finished filling the tank before she even left to get the coffee.

This prompts George to wrap up his conversation so they can get back on the road. But before he does so, there is one last question: *"How long does it take to recharge your car?"*

The driver nonchalantly lets George know that it is typically around 30-45 minutes. It all depends on the wattage and type of charging station. George thanks the driver and wishes him well on the rest of his journey.

George has so many more questions, but it is time to finish their pit stop and get back on the road. Back in the car, the family enjoys about an hour collectively reviewing vacation highlights before everyone starts to fall asleep one-by-one.

Once again, George is left alone with his thoughts. He thinks about the lack of concern so many in his industry have over electrified vehicles. He has only just started his research, but he has heard nothing to suggest that this threat isn't genuine.

George considers a worst-case scenario for his division. What if government regulation forced his industry to move to electrified vehicles. Unless the timeline was quite long, he could be in trouble considering the many capital equipment investments he has made in the last ten years.

The burden of his responsibilities to his parent company weighs heavy on George, but the burden of his responsibility to his workers and his community are what keep him up at night. He can't be the one that shuts off the lights on the company that has been the cornerstone of his community for over 100 years.

Regardless of what anyone else thinks, George knows what must be done. He must shore up his exposure to the electric vehicle trend and find opportunities that will support a future many are resistant to acknowledge.

# 31

## DO THE MATH!

One of the most important contexts in business is math. There are distinct advantages to having inputs and outcomes you can accurately and consistently measure. The first advantage is that there is less ambiguity when interpreting the reality of the situation. One hundred fifty pounds is the same in the United States as it is in the United Kingdom. This might seem trivial, but it is exceptionally important. We have a clear definition of what a pound is and agreed upon methods to measure it. In fact, the history of weights and measures are as old as recorded human history. We find references to weights and measures in the Bible, hieroglyphics, and almost every ancient text.

The second great advantage is the ability to track progress and improvement over time. As the old business mantra says, *"you can't improve what you don't measure."* Relative changes over time allow us to see trends and patterns that may correlate with new strategies, tactics, or policy changes. By using the scientific method to isolate variables, we can identify the impact of individual changes. And when we can correlate results to their stimuli, we open the door to learning and improvement.

For all the wonderful advantages that measurable facts bring into our analysis, there are some important limitations that must be discussed. Many of these are tied to concepts that we feel we already mastered in our formative education.

One of the more shocking limitations can be illustrated with the very simplistic skill of number sense. That is the skill of knowing that 10 is less than 20 and that 100 is greater than 30. However, just because we mastered that skill in first grade does not mean that it is transferable to all numbers.

Consider this: One million seconds is equivalent to twelve days. With that knowledge, what do we guess one billion seconds is equivalent to? When people hear that it is thirty-two years, they are often surprised. Isn't a billion the new million? However, when people hear that a trillion seconds is thirty-two thousand years, they frequently doubt the math because of the shocking difference.

I have given countless presentations to highly educated engineers, technology professionals, and statisticians and I'm always entertained by the audible gasps when these number equivalencies are revealed. It is important to accept that our understanding of what we know is often less than what we think.

Another common misconception is that there is only one right answer when we are dealing with numbers. Most of our formative education is predicated on the idea of finding the correct answer in any math problem. In the real world, however, there can be many right answers. Nowhere is this truer than in the field of accounting– the math of business.

In the world of business, there can often be multiple right answers. In large part this is due to the variety of interpretations, assumptions, and analytical methods available at our disposal. Just because we are presented with a number on a spreadsheet does not mean that we have arrived at some amazing ground truth that must be accurate.

The very best CFOs, auditors, and business analysts are wise to ferret out qualifying assumptions, biased interpretations, and subjective methods of data analysis. What can be easy to accept as fact is often a soupy combination of opinion and numbers.

Consider the generally accepted health guideline that 10,000 steps per day is the target goal for healthy living. We must be cognizant that this goal is structured for the "average" person. In actuality, what is right for each person may be very different. Additionally, there can be wide disparities on how specific devices take those measurements. Your smart watch may provide a different reading than your phone or a function-specific pedometer specifically set to your stride. The act of collecting data and drawing conclusions from said data can be very complicated and confusing. What we do know is that the 10,000-step guideline is useful in reducing overall health risks. What we cannot conclude is that 10,000 steps a day will prevent health issues.

In my work as a business advisor, I often find that people rely heavily on facts and figures to make their point. There is nothing wrong with the practice of strengthening a hypothesis with supporting data. Strangely, though, the eagerness to support a particular point of view often restricts the effort to fully qualify those facts or do the math that may surface inconsistencies.

If you pay close attention, a tragic comedy plays out in nearly every business meeting. In large part, this is due to the fact that most people generally don't enjoy math. As a result, meeting participants frequently shut down their critical thinking and blindly accept someone else's math. Very few people spend the time to understand how seemingly disparate facts buried within a meeting interact with one another. It is comical how many times the math supporting an argument just doesn't add up; and it is tragic how often faulty math is overlooked. In fact, sixty percent of the time you'll find that the math is flawed every time.

For as much as we don't enjoy math, there are comforting aspects that can't be denied. Math can comfort us by letting us know where we are. Have we saved enough for retirement? How close are we to meeting our sales targets?

Math can often be the perfect solution to help us calm emotions that tend to spiral out of control. With math, we can set limits to the fears that dominate our emotional state. Oddly enough, the unemotional discipline of math can be the ideal way to comfort our psyche, bolster our ego, and balance our thinking.

If there is one takeaway from this chapter, it is that the presence of numbers is not an inherent representation of fact. There is very rarely any "ground truth" in business. There are no "right" answers. But doing the math is an essential part of how we can understand the limits of any problem or the impact of our efforts. When we take the time to do the math, we may not find the "answer," but we can utilize numbers and statistics to increase our odds of success.

■ ■ ■

George is back in the office, refreshed and ready to go. Even though he has much on his mind, he is optimistic and energized. Perhaps this is because his team is fantastic at running the day-to-day operations leaving him the time to focus on the strategic direction of the company.

For several years that focus has been on a string of capital investments that helped his team lower costs to compete with the trend toward offshore component manufacturing. Their efforts have been successful, but George is hoping those investments don't leave him with fewer options for their next strategic hurdle: vehicle electrification.

George assembles his senior leadership team to discuss his concerns with the shift toward vehicle electrification. This won't be the first time this group has discussed this topic, but it will be the first time since George's renewed interest in the threat it poses to their division.

As a leader, George prefers to listen to the opinions of his team before he makes any comments. Over the years he has found that this is the best way for him to get authentic feedback and collaboration amongst his leadership team. Today is no different. George starts the meeting with a simple question: *"Should we be doing anything different when it comes to vehicle electrification?"*

The discussion is lively, wide-ranging, and passionate. Before George provides his input, he summarizes what he has heard from his team:

- The length of routes for the light-industrial market have increased by 17% in the past five years. Electric vehicles don't have the 500-mile range of gas-powered vehicles, making them a bad fit for the applications they serve.
- Electric vehicles take 8-12 hours to recharge and that is too long for light-industrial vehicles that can be in the field for more than 12 hours per day.
- Most electric vehicles are direct drive or single gear mechanisms. The applications of our customer base favor the high-torque, multi-gear solutions we produce.
- Electric vehicle transmissions tend to be inline and do not offer the same type of ground clearance that are required in the light-industrial space.

After reciting what he has heard, he asks his team another simple question: *"Am I to assume, based on these comments, that we don't need to do anything about vehicle electrification? Is electrification not a threat to our business?"*

One of the more senior members of his team pipes back, *"At this time George, I think we should just stay the course and see how this whole electric vehicle thing plays out."*

George isn't surprised by this answer, but he is disappointed. He then shifts into a tone of voice that gets the attention of his team, *"If that's the case, then I'd like to know the answers to these questions before we sit back and stay the course."*

- Are our customers' routes above 250 miles per day?
- What is the current range of most electric vehicles?
- How fast is electric vehicle range increasing each year?
- How old is that 8-12 hour charging time information?
- What is the growth rate of charging station availability?
- What is the growth rate of charging station capacity?
- Does that vary by region?
- Don't electric motors offer more torque?
- Are there any multi-gear electric motor vehicles?
- What is our customer's required ground clearance?

George had done his research and knew the answers to many of these questions. His team's commentary contained many contradictions, terrible assumptions and factual references that had no connection to the problem at hand. George could have called out his team for their inability to properly assess the situation, but he didn't do that. George wants something more from his team. He wants them to engage. He wants them to be involved in shaping the future of this company and the community that depends on them.

George recognizes their reluctance to the unwelcome change that is being thrust upon them. He acknowledges their fears with the following statement:

*"I know you're scared. This is new to all of us. Vehicle electrification could mean the end of what we've done here for over one hundred years. We have spent millions of dollars improving production to be domestically competitive and electric vehicles don't seem to need much of what is tooled and equipped to*

*manufacture. Volume decreases due to electrification could eliminate the cost advantages we have all worked so hard to achieve. But we must stop looking at this problem from our limited perspective. We need to look at what opportunities might result from this shift in technology."*

George then finishes with a bold statement to his team: *"Vehicle electrification is not a matter of **if**.. it is a matter of **when**. Let's start by concentrating our efforts on when?"*

# 32

## BALANCING EMOTIONS

The emotional portion of our brains control more of our internal narrative than we think. Perhaps Dale Carnegie said it best in 1936, a full thirty-three years before the Society for Neuroscience was formed.

> *"When dealing with people, let us remember we are not dealing with creatures of logic. We are dealing with creatures of emotion, creatures bristling with prejudices and motivated by pride and vanity."*

Most of us assume that the logical portion of our brain is what drives most of our decision making. And while our prefrontal cortex may arguably do plenty of heavy lifting, it is the emotional center of the brain that makes the final decision. In fact, modern neuroscience has shown that our decisions start and finish in the emotional center of our brain (Damasio, 1994). Furthermore, experiments have shown how people with damage to the emotion centers of their brain are incapable of making even the simplest of decisions. In essence, we are cognitively paralyzed without our emotions.

Any good trial lawyer understands that the facts only take you so far. It is the narrative that contains those facts and the emotional reactions of the jury that secures hearts and minds. Whether we observe them in the business world or in politics, we are frequently persuaded by people who can eloquently insert facts and memories into well-crafted narratives that stir our emotions. Perhaps that is why people gifted with the skill of storytelling and analogy tend to be the most persuasive.

It takes time and great discipline –the kind scientists use– to ensure that data is used properly. Every day, people create presentations and other data-driven talking points that are tragically flawed and doomed to provide misleading results. Even scientists struggle with the temptation to skew data to support a hypothesis. Surprisingly, facts and logic are often used to justify our emotional decisions more than they are used to reveal any new understanding.

Our ability to be influenced is a function of many instinctual tendencies that have allowed the human species to survive and thrive throughout the centuries. Dr. Robert Cialdini, also known as the "Godfather of Influence", has studied persuasion and influence for most of his career. His work highlights the many principles that guide effective persuasion as well as the cognitive limitations that allow our attention and interests to be hijacked by skillfully altering a recipient's perspective. His books are essential reading for anyone wishing to effectively exert any level of influence. Put simply, we are easily manipulated in ways that ironically contradict the enormous complexity of the human mind.

In fact, the profession that most expertly exploits the limitations of our cognitive function are magicians. They are masters of distraction, of altering perspective and of using our own minds to challenge deeply held beliefs. Anyone who has enjoyed the performance of a professional illusionist understands how they can get us to question the immutable laws of physics and the accurate functioning of our own physical senses.

Modern neuroscience and Nobel Prize-winning research has given us a window into the many cognitive biases and logical fallacies that misdirect our minds and interfere with our ability to accurately assess the world around us. There are approximately 185 cognitive biases that cloud and influence what we would otherwise consider rational judgment. One of the most pervasive cognitive biases is confirmation bias. This bias primes our minds to seek information that confirms our view of the world while simultaneously dismissing data that would contradict those views. We see other people doing this every day, but somehow, we consider ourselves immune from the influences of cognitive bias on our own flawless logic.

Sadly, our information-heavy data-driven world only makes these weaknesses more prevalent. Whether we are being inundated with emails or endless supplies of Internet-enabled data streams, we are continuously pushed to the limits of cognitive function. And while some people deal with cognitive overload more gracefully than others, everyone has their limit. When we reach these limits of cognition, our insidious hardwired biases exert even more pressure on our thinking (Yu, R., 2016; Allred, Crawford, Duffy, and Smith, 2014). Our biases engage to guide us down pathways that decrease the cognitive load on our brains. Like oil naturally separating from water, our innate tendencies offer simple explanations and tidy solutions that offer the clean cut of binary outcomes. Judgment becomes good or bad. Ideas become right or wrong. Problems become apocalyptic or insignificant. People become righteous or evil. Everything becomes *either-or*.

In reality, nearly all human interactions are a tangled mess of contradictions and half-truths with options and solutions that exist along a continuum. Details can be murky. Facts can oppose one another. Ideas can be both right and wrong. People are neither righteous nor evil. And even when we believe to have found the elusive fact-based "ground truth," our emotions still govern the final decision.

It is impossible to escape the iron grip that our emotions exert on our decision making. What we can do, however, is moderate the tendencies that push us too far in any one direction. As with any other extreme behavior we wish to control, it is important to start with awareness and acceptance. From there we can begin to address the innate temptations that drive us toward unproductive outcomes.

A very effective tool to help moderate emotions is humor. That is because humor typically pokes fun at extreme human conditions and behaviors. Humor is what soldiers use in the heat of battle to quell heightened emotions of fear and uncertainty. Humor can help us back off from the edges and migrate toward a more reasonable center. Humor helps bridge the gap between emotions and reality. It is no wonder that the best leaders typically have a way of using humor appropriately and in context.

We would not be human without our emotions and the strong pull they exert on our logical mind. The struggle between our emotional tendencies and our logical mind is a central theme of nearly every philosophy book ever written. But the goal of philosophy, psychology, or any pursuit of self-discovery is not to make us unemotional; the goal is to balance our emotions with our reason. Balance is what is needed. Balance is what is effective. Balance provides the most accurate view of the world around us. Balance allows us to find the clarity that reveals a clear path forward.

■ ■ ■

George knows what failure would look like. His worst fears are that his division is shut down because they do not deal with the challenge of vehicle electrification. George would be responsible for laying off over 3000 workers and 500 office personnel. And as the largest employer in the region, his community would likely experience a devastating blow that could change his hometown forever. Families he knows would be affected. Kids he has coached might not be able to afford college. Restaurants that know him by name might need to shut down. George knows that the Midwest is littered with towns that were once great. It is an outcome George cannot stomach.

Having spent too much time thinking about failure, George turns his attention to victory. What does victory look like?

Thinking about his immigrant grandfather, George imagines his own grandchildren attending a celebration for the bicentennial company anniversary. George isn't looking for glory, he just wants to play his role in a long tradition that started well before his time. For George, victory is a thriving company, a productive workforce, and a community with a secure future.

George understands that he is at the helm of this ship at a critical point in this company's journey. He feels the pressure of immense responsibility, but he fully appreciates the honor bestowed upon him to bear this burden. What troubles him is that he feels his senior leaders don't recognize the danger imposed by the "vehicle electrification iceberg" they are steaming toward.

George isn't looking to undermine his senior team, but he suspects that his leaders are too emotionally attached to the safety and consistency of their current business model. Realizing the need for a fresh perspective, George enlists the most creative people in the company– Department 817 . This is the department of clever engineers that implemented the capital improvements that helped the company stay competitive with domestic manufacturing. The engineers in 817 are not business strategists, but they are very creative, extremely clever, and exceptionally curious; exactly what is needed to meet this challenge.

George gathers the team from Department 817 into a large conference room. Without much warning and no agenda, the engineers are braced for bad news. As he enters the room, George is delighted that everyone is on edge. He wants them to be primed for the challenge they are about to receive:

*"The reason you are here is because legislation has just been proposed that will force our entire customer base to migrate to electric vehicles by next year. Lobbyists for our industry have confirmed that it is likely to pass."*

After a sizable pause in his delivery and many audible gasps from the engineers, George completes his thought:

*"I'm engaging you —the best problem solvers in the company— to think through this fictional scenario. While it may be unlikely that we will see such aggressive legislation, it is very likely that our industry is profoundly affected by vehicle electrification in the coming years. We must be prepared. I'd like for all of you to brainstorm ideas on how we deal with this threat to our business and our livelihoods."*

George gives them one week to brainstorm ideas before they meet again. For George, waiting to hear what they come up with is like counting down the days to Christmas.

When the day finally arrives, the room is filled with George, his senior leadership team and all of Department 817. Glen, the leader of Department 817, stands in front of the room and makes a surprising and bold statement:

*"Challenging problems like this are exactly why we all became engineers. In the last week, there were heated discussions coupled with incredibly innovative thinking. But as the week progressed, our newest team member had some of the best perspectives on this challenge. We all agree that he should be the one to share our collective insights."*

A tall, wiry, and nervous young man stands up to address his peers and the executive team. He wastes no time speaking his mind and clarifying his perspective:

*"I love being an engineer, but I haven't worked here long enough to really care about our gears and assemblies that much. I have no emotional attachment to them. In all our discussions I noticed a deep connection to our history, our recent capital projects, and our expertise with the products we currently manufacture. The longer we view inevitable changes as a threat to what we've already accomplished, the more we are missing the real point. This is a golden opportunity to work within a brand new and exciting design envelope."*

Several members of George's leadership team are staring at him wondering when he is going to shut this down. Perhaps this young upstart may not have understood his audience. But George –trusting Glen– is interested and curious as to where this is going. It certainly isn't what he expected.

Unfazed by the critical stares of the executive team, the young engineer continues his explanation:

*"My fishing buddies are all users of the vehicles that our products go into. When we talk about their trucks, they don't know anything about our gears and linkages. They only complain about the broader conditions that annoy them. They complain about hauling big generators everywhere. They need more ground clearance for the mud and ruts on jobsites. They need more torque at low speeds for difficult terrain, but they still need torque at high speeds for towing heavy loads. When emissions standards kicked in several years ago, the old diesel engines in their truck fleets were replaced with more fuel-efficient gas engines. They would much prefer their old diesel engines and they are scared to death of losing their gas engines.*

*The good news is that electric vehicles might be exactly what they want. An electric vehicle battery can replace heavy and cumbersome generators. Electric motors have a much better torque profile across different speeds. And when our team spoke about ground clearance, we hit a wall for a few days. But someone on our team suggested using portal axles like they do on the Humvees he used in the Army. They are generally too expensive and add enough weight to crush fuel economy targets. But with electric vehicles, emissions targets aren't an issue and the money that used to be spent on our transmission gears —the components electrification eliminates— could be used on the gearing and linkages for portal axles. We could help make a truck our end users love more than what they drive today."*

George thanks the entire team and ends the meeting with a note of gratitude. For a week's worth of work, their analysis is quite impressive. He cautions everyone to avoid jumping to any conclusions and suggests that they keep investigating these ideas further. It will be important to pressure test all assumptions and to make sure the math adds up.

George congratulates the young engineer and thanks him for his candor. He then seeks out Glen and thanks her for her leadership. This was a risky move for her and the whole department, but it was the perfect medicine for his team and the entire organization.

# 33

## THE KEY TO THE KINGDOM

There is a unique period in the development of most children that is often considered to be one of the most frustrating times for parents. At some point between ages two and four, many children begin a journey of discovery with the magical question of *why*.

Why is the sky blue?
Why do dogs bark?
Why do we have to eat our broccoli?

Parents may know the answer to some questions, but it does not take long for the incessant droning of *why* to hit upon topics of immense complexity, scientific discernment, or age-inappropriate context. However frustrating it is for parents, it is simultaneously impressive how quickly a three-year-old can push to the cognitive limits of an adult.

When you examine the situation from the perspective of the child, this is a profoundly empowering inflection point in their self-awareness. This is a time of unlimited discovery and insatiable curiosity. I would contend, albeit unscientifically, that this is the most important time in the development of a child's mind.

When we are quick to dismiss a child's curiosity with answers like –"*that's just the way it is*"– we do little to encourage a continued appetite for additional knowledge. It is only when we encourage children with actual engagement that we help them sharpen their curiosity and develop their intellect. Perhaps a better response is: *"That's a great question, let's find the answer together."*

I consider myself fortunate to have had parents that encouraged my curiosity and engaged with me in ways that allowed me to pursue knowledge and find the answers to my questions. I can only hope I have aided my own children as well as my parents supported me.

In fact, the most important modeling for me was when my parents shared how they were also interested in understanding how something worked. Learning with someone is always better than learning alone. Thinking partners add diversity and context that is challenging to develop in isolation.

As a society, we congregate in schools and universities to advance our understanding and increase our collective knowledge. As individuals, however, we often distract ourselves with diplomas, certifications, and degrees designating our command of particular disciplines. And while mastery is an honorable pursuit, it is also a dangerous objective. Mastery once claimed is immediately obsolete. To assume otherwise is to accept that creativity has been exhausted, innovation has stalled and all that is possible has been illuminated. Mastery cannot exist as a finite achievement.

There is a saying within the military's elite special operations units: *"Selection is an ongoing process."* One does not forever operate at an elite level because they once did during their initial selection. To remain a member of an elite unit, you must continuously demonstrate the capacity to operate at the appropriate level.

The same can be said for anyone seeking knowledge, wisdom, or clarity. These are goals that can never be fully realized. There is always more knowledge, greater wisdom, or improved clarity to be acquired.

Remember that the world was once flat and that cigarettes were once considered good for your health. Socrates' words are as prescient today as they were over two thousand years ago,

---

*"The only true wisdom is in knowing you know nothing."*

---

This is where the impact of curiosity comes into sharp focus. Without curiosity, knowledge develops finite boundaries. Without curiosity, hope cannot exist. Curiosity is the fuel that powers all future opportunities. Curiosity is the inspiration for questions and the motivation for understanding. Curiosity is what makes some people persist when others quit. Curiosity is the catalyst that drives a deeper understanding that surfaces the why behind the how.

The temptation to stop the process of discovery once you start getting results is incredible. Only the truly committed persist in their quest for deeper understanding. Very few ever learn the why behind the how:

- The incurious mind does not independently seek feedback on its performance– it waits for feedback.
- The incurious mind has trouble discerning how other people's motivations can differ from its own.
- The incurious mind is satisfied with symptoms and neglects the effort to search for root causes.
- The incurious mind struggles with empathy because it cannot imagine how another person may be impacted by a decision or circumstance.
- The incurious mind prevents a growth mindset because it will never wonder what is beyond the next horizon.
- The incurious mind does not ask questions, nor does it listen.

- The incurious mind finds answers in the shallows and avoids the richer treasure offered in the depths.
- The incurious mind has finite potential.

As Plutarch so wisely stated centuries ago,

---

*"The mind is not a vessel to be filled, but a fire to be kindled."*

---

Curiosity is the key that unlocks all the other positive behaviors. Context may be the king, but curiosity is the key to the kingdom.

■ ■ ■

George gathers his leadership team together and asks them what they thought of the presentation. He is curious to know how they received the analysis presented by the team in Department 817.

The senior leader who spoke up in their original meeting –the one that said they should wait to see how things play out– was the first to speak. With a tone of deep humility, he described how the nervous young engineer made him question his earlier position. He never realized how emotionally attached he had become to the comfortable world they have built through the years. In a moment of uncharacteristic vulnerability, he said he was shocked to realize how his viewpoint began to orbit around the company rather than the broader ecosystem in which their company is only a small part.

Another leader also commented on the impact of the Department 817 engineers. She stated how she hadn't realized how much she had lost her creative edge. It was as if there was some unwritten rule that the curious and creative portion of her mind could not coexist with her management responsibilities. What was most shocking to her was that this false limitation was entirely self-imposed. With that in mind, she found new inspiration and came up with some additional ideas to pursue.

As she considered the specific challenge of the muddy job sites their customers encounter, she realized that it might be easier to implement four-wheel steering with an electric drivetrain. Four-wheel steering would be very helpful in muddy environments and would require gearing like what they produce today. In fact, greater capability in rougher terrain may help them reach international markets where infrastructure is less developed.

At that moment something interesting happened around the conference room table. Eyes widened and heads tilted upward as everyone imagined what four-wheel steering would look like on a job site. With one creative idea, the permission she had given herself had just been transferred to everyone in the room. Her curiosity was a catalyst for the senior team just as the Department 817 engineers were a catalyst for her.

The idea immediately prompted a lively discussion among the senior leadership team. Questions raced back and forth across the table. And while questions were not an uncommon occurrence in these meetings, these types of questions were. None of the questions were judgmental or skeptical in nature. All the questions were filled with excitement and focused on possibility.

George was thrilled to see his team collaborate in a way that seemed like they were all new to the company and their jobs. There was an air of youthful enthusiasm that had been missing for some time. George was proud of how he had jump started his management focused team into a more strategic and creative mindset. Quietly, though, George knows that they only settled into their more conservative mindset because of his leadership. George makes a mental note to carefully monitor the impact of his leadership.

Wary of casting a shadow over this lively discussion, George's Chief Financial Officer speaks up with some sobering comments:

*"I hate to be the one to rain on this parade, but we have some real challenges with this transition. The many capital investments we have made to compete domestically are predicated on volumes and throughput that need to keep pace with our growth projections. Financially, we're a bit too sensitive to fluctuations in production capacity. I'm not saying we can't make this kind of transition, but I am saying that it will require tremendous precision in our execution."*

George acknowledges that this situation is as complex as the gears and linkages they create for vehicles. There are a lot of moving parts, but there is a path forward if they work together. They need to do the research and the math necessary to formulate a plan that is properly sequenced to maintain profitability and maximize long-term potential. They will need to act on what they can do now and be patient to make changes as the market and their parent company permit. It will be a delicate balancing act.

Pleased with the collaboration of his team, George knows that it won't mean anything if they don't walk away with action items and responsibility assignments on the important items they need to investigate. After a short discussion, George documents the following assignments of responsibility:

- The VP of marketing will lead research into the needs and opportunities of their ultimate end-users.
- The VP of engineering will direct teams investigating the viability of both portal axles and four-wheel steering.
- The VP of operations will examine how their existing tooling and equipment can be used to make the new products engineering is investigating.
- The VP of business development will determine which partners and customers will be critical to work with as they bring some of their new ideas to market.

- The CFO will investigate the sensitivity of their financial projections to identify what can be done to improve their flexibility with the new strategy.
- And George will find a partner that can help them understand and track EV battery capacity and range projections as well as charging station capacity, geographic density, and growth.

George concludes the meeting with the following statement: *"We should be proud of what we have accomplished, but not so proud that we are blinded by our success. Many of us started our careers as engineers, much like the young man who has opened our eyes. It is time for us to renew our curiosity like all the engineers that drive innovation in Department 817. The future of our company and our community depends upon clear-eyed thinking from this management team. Success is not a destination we can claim we have reached; it is a narrow path of focused effort that never ends.*

*We need to seek the information that will give us greater context and understanding of our situation. We need to pressure test all our assumptions. We need to do the math that will allow us to balance our near-term profitability with our long-term success. We need to be mindful of how our emotions influence our actions. We cannot let our contentment, or our fears, limit our options. However, we should engage our passion for this company and our community to energize our efforts. Lastly, let's make sure we are looking at our situation from all angles. There is hope for the future of our company, but it will be guided by the depth of our creativity and judged by our ability to balance many competing interests. Let's get to work."*

# 34

## GEORGE'S BALANCING ACT

For as good as George feels about the renewed energy within his business, the enormity of the situation is gnawing at him. Ironically, his problem is that his company is currently very healthy and profitable. As the darling of the conglomerate that purchased his organization ten years ago, nobody wants to consider that there could be an existential threat to their dominant market position. But George knows better. His ship is headed into icy waters. Dangerous icebergs –in the form of vehicle electrification– are on the horizon.

In the last five years, much of George's political capital was spent trying to preserve the economy of his hometown by improving their domestic manufacturing competitiveness. And while his strategy has proven to be wildly profitable, George has an uphill battle trying to convince his parent company that there is a new problem that requires near-term action to mitigate. Regardless of the financial benefit, there is a legitimate fear that George has exhausted his "line of credit" with the parent company.

Beyond that, George still can't define exactly what the threat is, how it will manifest itself or when it will start to impact the business. George's instincts have always served him well, but he knows that he needs more data and critical analysis to make his case.

Realizing that the required analysis is best suited for an outside consultant, George reaches out to an old friend from college. Gary is a former roommate and fraternity brother that has been working in consulting for most of his career. After thirty minutes revisiting embarrassing moments from their past, the two get down to business. George describes his situation and asks Gary to point him in the right direction.

Unlike the disorganized and undisciplined "brother" he had in college, Gary quickly pivots into consultant mode and asks several very insightful questions.

- *What are the very first specific events you would observe that would turn vehicle electrification from a fear into a real threat to your business?*
- *Assuming that EV transitions are a threat, when do you think your customers and usage with their end-customers will begin eroding your volumes?*
- *How much volume erosion can you absorb before your financials turn South or your parent company loses confidence in you?*
- *How much time do you need to prepare and implement new production lines with products that can backfill your volumes?*

George didn't have the answers to these questions, but he is amazed at how quickly Gary was able to zero in on the issues that need to be addressed. His internal team was focused on their reaction and potential solutions, but Gary seemed to understand higher-level issues that are also very important. Gary's line of inquiry addresses the concerns that will mirror those of his parent company.

*"That was amazing, Gary,"* stated an awestruck George.

*Gary responds: "Listen, George… I've been doing this a long time. We could analyze this situation forever. Honestly, that's what most people do. But when you need to get to the core issue fast, all your questions need to address more than one context. In most cases, time-based contexts or sequence-based contexts are particularly helpful.*

*You need to think fast like an NFL quarterback about to change a play. What is the defense telling me with the way they are lined up? How will that affect how much time I have? And finally, how can I use that time as wisely as possible to have the most success. That's the same thing we are doing here.*

*What are the triggers that will confirm any assumptions we have made? How much time will we have while this scenario plays out? And what signs do we need to recognize that will signal an opening for decisive action?"*

George knew Gary had been very successful in his career, but he had yet to experience his proficiency in action. Impressed with his consulting expertise, George asks Gary if his firm can help him with his EV investigation project.

Gary lets George know that his firm does do some of this consulting and they certainly can help. But knowing how important and critical this project is to George, his company, and his community, Gary declines;

*"George, you need to hire the very best for this project. We can do a good job for you… but the stakes are too high to get someone who will just do a good job. You need to work with W.W. Consulting. I'll make an introduction for you. I just hope they have the bandwidth to help."*

After thanking Gary for his help, George sits quietly at his desk contemplating his situation. He is no longer pondering particular solutions; he is thinking about a pathway to implement some improved solution that has yet to be identified. George needs a strategy. And that strategy will need to be carefully executed so that the profitability of his business is not affected. George realizes that it's one thing to be curious about the future, but it is a whole different level to be curious about how you are going to deal with the future.

With the helpful introduction from Gary, George secures a meeting with W.W. Consulting. As promised, the team from WWC is top notch. They ask many of the same questions that Gary asked, and they dig even deeper. In particular, they are very keen to clarify any assumptions in George's story. They are also very good at asking data-oriented questions enabling them to make quick calculations that confirm the continuity of George's statements. They certainly feel like the best of the best.

Based on their discussion, George gets the feeling that his intuition is accurate. Electrification will indeed affect his business. A successful outcome of this project will be data that will confirm and estimate the impact to his business. Additionally, he expects to learn the timing of when electrification should begin to affect his business and when he needs to have countermeasures in place to assure consistent profitability for his parent company.

Feeling confident that WWC is indeed the firm to work with, George commissions the project. And while he is relieved that he is on the right path, he is not happy about having to wait three months for the project to be completed.

With his team working on four-wheel steering, portal axles and other creative innovations, George is surprised that the three months go so quickly. And while he is eager to get the results of the study he commissioned; he also knows he is three months closer to the vehicle electrification iceberg.

The final report and the team he commissioned are as professional as he had hoped. The findings do confirm that vehicle electrification will have a significant impact on his business. Without any response to participate in the shift toward electrification, George's company and his hometown could become another sad, midwestern story.

What stands out to George are the following facts:

- The analysis indicates that EV models will start to be introduced in about 2 model years or 36 months.
- Their customer base needs a 400-mile range between charges to be an effective alternative.
- To replace generators, a 500-mile range battery would be necessary.
- Battery technology should reach the 400-mile range at around 48 months and 500 miles at 60 months.
- Volumes will not be impacted significantly until the 400-mile range batteries are available.
- Based on the information available today, WWC is 95% confident that these timelines will not be longer but only 50% confident that they are not shorter.
- WWC relates that how long it takes to charge a battery will not be as big a factor as compared to where high wattage charging stations are located. Charging station growth and geographic saturation will likely be the controlling factor that influences adoption.

Learning a lesson or two from Gary, George has some of his own tough questions for the WWC team: *"So, we have your stated confidence levels as of today. What happens to your confidence levels as time progresses? Do they get more accurate or less accurate?"*

The response George receives is not what he expected, but it is exactly what he needed to hear;

*"George, the estimates we make today will become less accurate with time. Based on the current trajectory of battery technology and EV adoption, we are relatively confident that our upper limit numbers are accurate. However, since every university in the world is working on battery technology and every government wants to benefit economically from this shift… we must assume that our lower end numbers –how soon this is going to happen– may decrease. However, we are 95% confident that vehicle electrification will significantly impact your*

*current production volumes in five years. We estimate the impact to be between 20 and 30 percent of your current production capacity."*

A twenty percent decrease in capacity would be devastating to his company and his community. It will be difficult to predict when it will happen and how much time he has to respond. Even more difficult will be the balancing act of carefully shifting some of his production capacity to EV products without affecting the traditional products that are their bread and butter. Getting the timing right will make all the difference. If George moves too soon, his company will suffer financially and not have the momentum to complete the transition. If he moves too slow, a competitor may seize the opportunity to dominate this new market.

George then asks another question to the folks from WWC: *"Is there any way you can continuously feed us this information so I can have up-to-date reports on the progress and probabilities of EV adoption? I will need this to make sure we don't move too early or miss our opportunity."*

The answer George receives is disconcerting. As sophisticated as they seem, the WWC team does most of their analysis with spreadsheets and human data gathering. While they appreciate George's request, they can only update the data every two months and by the time they present their report, the results may be as much as four months old.

The emotional burden of this transition is stressing George as if he is Atlas shouldering the weight of his entire company and community. The stakes are high, and he must be perfect with the timing of this transition. With that said, George understands the constraints and the complexity that the WWC team is dealing with. Their response makes sense, but it frustrates him beyond his capacity to contain his emotions.

In an uncharacteristic and impulsive outburst in front of the entire WWC team and his senior leadership, George unloads with an emotional monologue that sends a strong message to everyone in the room:

*"Your report is exactly what we asked for and totally useless! By the time you all get back to your offices these findings are less valuable than they are right now. We paid a fortune to get the very best in the industry and this is not what I expected. I feel like you are selling me yesterday's newspaper at the same price I'd pay for a sneak peek on tomorrow's headlines!*

*"I'm thankful for what we've learned… but this will not help me calm my nerves or time our transition. It certainly won't help us convince our parent company to accelerate dealing with these very real threats to our business. We don't need to know about some change we all know will happen… we need to know about the rate of change —the velocity— of these transitions. If we are to initiate a response and accelerate our activity, we need consistent and timely updates on the point in time result you just presented.*

*"I'm not sure if you realize this, but an entire community depends on us getting this right. I expect more… In fact, I demand more. From what I've been told you are the best of the best. Prove it!"*

# PART IV

## SEQUENCING & TIMING

In the Fall of 1989, I was a ninth semester Mechanical Engineering student at the University of Illinois in Urbana-Champaign. I was finally about to graduate. As a once proud high school honor student, I had battled semester after semester just to stay in the program. The difficult curriculum would naturally cull the herd each semester, eventually leaving only the most grizzled veterans. I survived. Barely.

Engineers from the University of Illinois were heavily recruited. Job interviews were plenty; less so for those of us who had descended to the bottom of the class through attrition. My classmates in the "Golden 100 Honor Society" (the bottom 100 people in my graduating class) experienced a soul-crushing abundance of rejection.

Early one evening, I found myself drinking a beer and playing Nintendo when my fraternity brother Dave entered my room with a ridiculous request. He asked me to stop drinking my beer, turn off the video game and put on a suit and tie. He was headed to a preparatory information seminar for a company he was interviewing with the next day. Dave was on the interview schedule because he was smart and in-demand. He had helped me pass countless classes and was likely trying to help me get out of my funk.

Still, his request seemed absurd. I wasn't even on the interview schedule. However, it was clear he was pretty excited about this company, so he continued to press the issue. Sensing my disinterest, he countered with an offer to buy the first pitcher of beer after the seminar. Minutes later, I was in my suit and ready to support Dave for a few hours.

We sat through a company overview and very impressive presentations by three Allen-Bradley executives. Most attendees took copious notes and prepared intelligent questions for their interviews the next day. At the conclusion of the event, each of the company executives migrated to a separate corner of the room to field questions.

Dave made a beeline across the room to the Human Resources representative. I picked the executive closest to me. Anxious to impress, candidates jockeyed for position to ask their discerning questions. With no horse in this race, I stood in the back and listened patiently as my executive thoughtfully addressed each candidate.

The crowd slowly thinned as candidates asked their questions and proceeded to leave. I glanced across the room and spied Dave still engaged in conversation. I thought it must be going well for him. In time, I found myself as the only student left in front of a very impressive gentleman by the name of Neal Keating.

Mr. Keating complimented me for being so patient and was curious to know what my lingering question must be. He figured it had to be good as many questions had already been asked by my peers. In what would become one of the most pivotal moments of my life, I didn't know what to do except to tell him the truth.

I recounted my story of the past several hours and Mr. Keating seemed to find it quite comical. I let him know how impressed I was with the company and began to sell him on how great Dave was. It was a natural conversation and I started to believe that Allen-Bradley must indeed be the employer of choice.

In a moment I shall never forget, Mr. Keating asked me what I was doing the next morning. I had no plans. He suggested that if I were to be at the interview location at 7:15 he would personally interview me before his first scheduled appointment at 8am. I thanked him with "Christmas morning" giddiness and proceeded to collect my fraternity brother. Naturally, there was reason to celebrate with a few beers... but only a few.

As fate would have it, I ended up working at Allen-Bradley in Milwaukee, Wisconsin. It was there that I met some of my best friends, and through them my wife. And without that chance introduction to Neal Keating so many years ago, the crazy chain of events that led to my beautiful family never would have happened.

I'm not one to discount hard work, strong values, talent, or perseverance. But I do recognize that sometimes it is just as important to have good timing.

Timing is very different from luck. Luck happens without choice. Timing is a dynamic construct. And to have good timing involves a decision to engage. Everyone in this story made choices to seize opportunities that were not obvious or part of the "plan."

On any given day we are presented with opportunities we don't see or fail to capitalize on. People with great timing are often seen as lucky, but great timing is a belief in opportunity; the patience to look for it and the willingness to seize it.

This section is about the importance of patience, timing, and the sequencing of events. All of these are essential components of any sound business strategy and are important contextual elements for the development of your own clarity.

# 35

## YOU CAN'T DO THIS ALONE

It's a strange thing for Diana to have placed prominently in her office. As a female CEO, this item might seem out of place on her desk, but for Diana it has great meaning. The item is a wooden plaque that her grandfather carved for her when she started her company. Beautifully engraved in the dark walnut wood is the title of a poem her grandfather would recite to her: *"No Man is an Island."*

The meaning and message of the quote transcends any interpretation of misogyny that could be ascribed to sixteenth century poet John Donne. On the day she received this gift from her grandfather, she knew what he was trying to tell her— *you can't do this alone*.

Diana thinks about her grandfather frequently; and when she is struggling, she tends to think about him and his advice even more. Today is one of those days.

Diana has just come out of the worst meeting she had had in many years. Her biggest client, and one of her favorite new leaders, has just issued a challenge to her and her team. Diana is not afraid of challenges, but this one is different. Her client called her team out for missing the mark on what they needed. They were contracted to perform a complex analysis, but they really didn't deliver the consulting that was necessary. They did not hear the unspoken pain or interpret the real need hidden in plain sight. Diana is ashamed that she was so focused on her business that she forgot about the "Art of Consulting" she often talks about with her team. She owns this failure.

As she looks at the inscription on the plaque, she realizes she needs help. There is no way she can meet this challenge without some additional insights. The problem is that she doesn't know where to turn.

Without many ideas, Diana turns to her mother-in-law for advice. Even though her professional career ended long before Dean was born, she has an amazing talent for networking with everyone she meets. In fact, they often joke that she may be more connected than Kevin Bacon.

Diana shares the nature of her predicament and is amazed at how effortlessly her mother-in-law finds a good person to speak with. In this case, the connection is painfully obvious and close to home… Diana's best friend, Nancy. It just so happens that Nancy's husband works in private equity and may know people that can help with Diana's predicament.

Eager to help, Nancy's husband Nick introduces Diana to a new VP they hired to drive sales in one of their portfolio companies. Nick interviewed her and remembered that her prior firm had software that sounded like it could benefit Diana and her firm. Nick makes the introduction which leads to a wonderful conversation and yet another introduction. It seems like a wild goose chase, but Diana knows how this works. Those who actively network realize opportunities that others expect to fall in their lap.

Diana is now speaking with a gentleman by the name of Sam. Sam is the VP of sales for a software company that helps its customers model complex business scenarios that are constantly changing. On the surface, this looks like a perfect fit.

Diana describes how she needs a better way to gather and monitor data that changes very frequently. Her client wants constant updates on the advancements of battery capacity, charging station proliferation, environmental tax incentives, regulations, and regional power grid stability to name a few. On top of that, he is requesting that they coordinate that data with their production schedules, capacity throughput, engineering projections, and new product introductions. Diana understands the rationale for her client's demanding request, but the complexity and timeliness of the effort is beyond her team's capacity to deliver. She needs a new way of approaching this problem.

After listening carefully and asking many great questions, Sam lets Diana know that his software is exactly what Diana needs. But before she can celebrate, Sam informs Diana that his company is buried with too many custom jobs. While Sam appreciates Diana's predicament, his own situation is something he must consider.

Sam then shares the challenges he is having with his business. As the new sales leader he is expected to make a turnaround, but it will be impossible unless he adopts a more scalable model for his business. He needs to focus on targeted industry problems with standardized models that will serve a number of different clients. Without this more uniform approach, Sam knows he doesn't stand a chance.

Disappointed but not discouraged, Diana shifts her perspective to a different context– Sam's. Putting on her consulting hat, she begins to ask Sam more questions about his challenges. Diana is curious about the characteristics of an ideal targeted industry and standardized model.

Sam recognizes where Diana is going and challenges her approach; *"Diana, I see where you are going, and I appreciate the effort. I just don't see how your situation is appropriate for one of our standardized models. The scenario you have described is far too customized for what I need right now."*

Not willing to give up, Diana goes into sales mode: *"But Sam, the environmental concerns and transitions my firm deals with are important to nearly every business in the world right now. You could hardly find a more common set of issues to model. Our industry is booming, and it will provide a rich pipeline to hit your sales targets. And on top of it all, we would be using your software to address one of the greatest problems we face as a human race."*

It's that last part that gets Sam's attention. Diana was careful to do her research before she met with Sam. She had studied many interviews with Sam's genius CEO and how he wants to solve all of the world's toughest problems. She had carefully inserted his exact phrasing into her pitch:

*"Diana, I'm impressed with your sales skills. You make a compelling case. But the situation you described is just too complex and unique to become one of our standard models."*

Diana replies to Sam with the following compromise, *"Sam, maybe we can help one another. I agree that my particular situation is too complex. But I can help identify the most common elements to help you create a model that will work for everyone in my industry. On top of that, I'll loan you one of my top consultants David to help build the models with you. He is great with numbers. If we can use your models to merely cut our work in half, we will have received tremendous benefit. But here's the key, by selling to consulting companies like mine, you can sell once and transact many times. We have dozens of active clients, all of whom could benefit from an instance of one of your models.... What do you think?"*

*"Diana, this is a big gamble for me and my family, but I like the way you think. I have a feeling we can be successful if we partner on this project— but the key is partnering. I hope you are looking out for me as much as you are looking out for your pressing client needs. I have no way of knowing that for sure... but I trust you. Together I think we can do this."*

That evening Diana thanks her mother-in-law for her help and guidance. Without her initial recommendation, she would not have found Sam or his amazing software. Her mother-in-law replies, *"Always remember, Diana, new friends make the world and all of its problems smaller."*

# 36

## SEQUENCING

A busy executive was on her way to work one morning when a white work van ran through a red light smashing violently into her luxury sedan. Airbags deployed, bumpers disintegrated, and steel buckled to absorb the tremendous impact. Both cars spun wildly, showering the intersection with thousands of fragments of plastic and glass.

Traffic stopped in all directions while shocked commuters called 9-1-1 for emergency assistance. It was clear that both vehicles would be needing critical lifesaving attention.

As the first responders approached the luxury sedan, it was clear that the woman inside was stunned and in shock from the impact. The damage was extensive and the EMT's were prepared for a heightened level of trauma.

The executive was conscious and aware of her situation but was clearly dealing with the clouded thinking that accompanies a severe concussion. Emergency personnel quickly recognized that she was suffering from a facial laceration and a compound fracture in one of her legs. Based on experience, they also knew that internal bleeding and possible cranial swelling could further complicate the driver's condition.

The police officer calmly let her know that help was on its way and that she was going to be okay. She nodded in acknowledgment but was still struggling to establish her own situational awareness. Moments later, a paramedic arrived on the scene and began to ask her questions to assess her condition. The paramedic was careful to ask yes or no questions she could answer with a nod of her head.

As she began to say *"Thank you,"* she realized she couldn't. Panic set in. Her front teeth were missing. As she impulsively scanned the automobile for her teeth, she noticed blood on the remnants of the deployed airbag and all over her silk blouse. She yelled out to the paramedic, *"My teef! My teef!"*

The paramedic was well aware of her dental trauma as soon as he arrived at the vehicle. This is why he was careful to ask questions that she could answer by nodding. As they loaded her into the ambulance, he calmed her by saying, *"Your teeth will be fine. Let's just get you to the hospital and we'll fix you right up."*

Once at the hospital, the ER staff quickly assessed her situation. They followed the standard protocols for this type of trauma situation. Stop Bleeding. Maintain blood pressure. Maintain airways and breathing. Evaluate for further trauma (internal bleeding, brain hemorrhage, etc.) before addressing less critical issues like the cosmetic facial trauma.

Dean was the attending ER physician and was leading the effort to evaluate the patient. CAT scans indicated that there was no cranial swelling, but she did have mild internal bleeding that required emergency surgery.

Hours later, Dean was making his rounds to see the executive in the recovery area. The executive's husband was seated next to her holding her hand. Dean comforted them with the good news that the internal bleeding had been addressed. With her most serious health concern resolved, they were also able to stabilize her leg. Unfortunately, a secondary surgery by an orthopedic surgeon would be necessary to ensure she would heal properly. Dean also shared that a plastic surgeon was available and did a wonderful job with her facial laceration. *"Overall,"* Dean said, *"you are very fortunate."*

Dean then asked them if they had any questions. This prompted the executive to hand her husband a note she had scrawled out on a notepad. The husband carefully read the note to himself before he commented to Dean:

*"Thank you for all of your life saving efforts. My wife and I are very grateful. However, she is very concerned about her front teeth. Did the paramedics recover her teeth at the scene? When and how will she be able to fix her front teeth? Is there an oral surgeon at the hospital? Can they repair or replace her teeth?"*

The executive nodded vigorously as if to emphasize how important these questions were to her.

This was not the first time Dean had seen patients respond this way. Patients often have a difficult time reconciling new health priorities that have been thrust upon them. Just this morning, having front teeth at a business meeting would have been a top priority. A few hours and an accident later, she should consider herself lucky to be breathing on her own.

Dean calmly answered their questions about the teeth. They had not been recovered at the scene. Even if the paramedics had found her teeth, the window to replace them had passed while they addressed her more serious injuries.

Dean assured them that she would be able to work with an oral surgeon to get a temporary partial and eventually proper dental implants. The process may take some time, but she is very fortunate considering the accident description the responding police officers had provided.

Dean tried to focus their attention on her leg and the physical therapy she would be needing after her next surgery. It would be some time before she was going to be back in the office.

The husband understood the explanation and thanked Dean. At some level, the executive also understood, but her eyes revealed a sadness that was inescapable.

When Dean arrives home late Friday night the twins are already in bed. After visiting their room to see his little ones peacefully sleeping, Dean returns to the kitchen anxious to share this story with Diana.

Diana pours two glasses of wine as Dean begins to recall the events of the last 24 hours. The story is captivating. Both Diana and Dean can't help but imagine how this would affect their family if it had been one of them driving to work.

Even with full knowledge of the situation and a dispassionate perspective, Diana is similarly mortified about the thought of losing her front teeth. Most of Diana's questions center around this topic. This prompts Dean to go into more detail on how the order in which you do things is what really matters in trauma situations.

After a few minutes, he notices that he has lost his wife's attention as she seems to be consumed by other thoughts. Familiar with this pattern of behavior, Dean asks Diana what she is thinking;

*"Thank you. This is exactly what I needed. It's the sequencing of events that I need to focus on to help George. All the things he needs to focus on are important, but everything is not important right now. If I can sequence things properly, this problem will get much more manageable for both my team and his."*

# 37

## TIMING

George is arriving at the airport early as he always does. It's the start of a long day as he travels to meet Diana, the CEO of the consulting firm he hired. Diana contacted him a few days earlier regarding the challenge he posed at the conclusion of their last meeting. She stated that she might have a solution, but that she would prefer discussing the matter in person. Anxious to learn more about Diana and her company, George suggested that they meet at her offices. If the future of his company —and perhaps his hometown— relies upon this boutique environmental consulting firm, George figured that he should get a closer look at their operation.

As George relaxes in his exit row seat, he marvels at the technology of the huge jet that is transporting him and several hundred other people on their short flight. He is amazed by the relative comfort they enjoy while traveling around 500 miles per hour. But before George can finish reading his newspaper, the plane lurches forward slightly and a recognizable sound echoes through the cabin as complex mechanisms manipulate the flaps to change the shape of the wing. It is a predictable sequence of events that always signals the plane is nearing its destination.

It is at this moment that George has an epiphany. He needs to stop trying to predict the future and pay attention to the changes that signal the future. The plane slowing and the sounds of the flaps extending are the leading indicators that the plane will be landing soon. In fact, those events happen well before the flight crew even announces they are preparing to land. George realizes that this may be the key to timing the delicate shift he foresees for his business.

With a drive that is nearly as long as his flight, Diana has arranged for a private limousine to transport George from the airport to her office. Diana sends Pavel, the driver she always uses when she travels. He is personable, professional, and timely. Diana wants to make sure George has a first-class experience heading into her offices.

Excited about his revelation, George can't wait to share this new perspective. He runs his ideas by Pavel to see if they sound reasonable. Pavel listens carefully and responds with the wisdom of a seasoned professional:

*"What you are describing sounds a lot like how I view the flow of traffic. My clients expect me to be on time. Nobody wants to be left waiting at the airport or worry about missing a flight. The system I use to track arrivals and departures is critical to dealing with flight delays and properly scheduling pickups. That system is simple and very accurate. The navigation system I use helps quite a bit, but the traffic information is often too old to give me actionable feedback. And if you are on the road, you can't wait to see an accident to adjust your route. You need to heighten your awareness as soon as you notice a slowdown in traffic. When you observe a change in the flow of the traffic that doesn't seem normal... that is when I start looking for options."*

George and Pavel continue their discussion for the remainder of the trip. He is fascinated by Pavel's insights and thanks him for his valuable input. It isn't even 9 AM and George has found inspiration in the most unlikely places.

Diana greets George and her friend Pavel as they arrive at the WWC offices. It is a friendly and warm welcome that sets the tone for a productive day. As they enter the building, they head straight into a large conference room that is the showcase of the office. Diana introduces George to Sam, who is already seated behind a laptop. After the requisite introductions and friendly greetings, Diana begins the session with the following statement:

*"Each of us is facing a unique problem we cannot solve on our own. However, the three of us have the potential to collaborate and solve our problems together."*

Diana relates Dean's car crash story to both Sam and George. She explains how the problem seems big in totality but can be more manageable when it is broken into its logical elements. All they need to do is identify the critical elements that must be decided first and which are the less important elements like the front teeth.

As the newcomer to the dialogue, Sam asks George many questions and then explains how his software works. Sam is keen to point out that modeling requires discipline. If you try to use all available information you can get bogged down in details and complexity that can confuse the powerful algorithms in the software. The best way to leverage the power of his product is to identify a focused set of relevant information that drives outcomes and decision making.

The team then spends several hours discussing and identifying the critical data elements for George's decision-making calculus. It is a discussion filled with challenging ideas and varied perspectives. When it is all said and done, the team feels good about their targeted data sets.

Sam adds to their confidence by stating that more relevant data allows the software to arrive at conclusions more quickly and with greater accuracy. Furthermore, from Diana's perspective, the data they have identified is universal to challenges all her clients are facing.

And while it seems like all the pieces of the puzzle are falling into place, something is troubling George. They are missing the element of changing velocity that he realized on the plane and confirmed with Pavel.

This line of discussion sends them down a path of discovery that reveals opportunities for each of them. The team quickly realizes that a change in the velocity of EV adoption may help surface the perfect timing for George's transitions. Furthermore, they surmise that subtle fluctuations in specific supply-chain metrics may also be leading indicators of broader change. With these new insights, George will have a better sense of when he might need to be prepared for impacts to his business. Diana now realizes that the rate of change component is more valuable to her clients than the static reports she has been developing over the last several years. Lastly, Sam sees a completely new capability that increases the value to his clients by a factor of ten.

And while this collaboration has filled them all with energy, George still has a lingering concern. Even with an early warning, he might not have enough time to re-tool his business to seize the opportunity for EV transmissions, portal axles, or four-wheel steering.

*"George, ever since you told me about your company and how much you care about your community I've been thinking about this problem,"* Diana responds. *"What if we didn't need to be as precise with our timing? What if we look at the transition from a standpoint of abundance rather than scarcity? There is no need to wait for one part of the business to decline before we promote newer product offerings. We can start right now. The opportunity to introduce portal axles and four-wheel steering does not depend on electrification. Some of the restrictions we have imposed upon ourselves are unnecessary."*

Initially, George is embarrassed by this self-imposed limitation that constrained him and his team into a zero-sum game mindset.

Perhaps this is exactly what the young engineer from department 817 was suggesting. But instead of feeling guilty, George is liberated by the burden it has lifted from his shoulders and offers this sincere response;

*"Diana, you are a special person. I truly enjoy working with you. I can't tell you how much I appreciate your personal investment in the future of my firm and my community. Thank you for today. I have renewed confidence in the future of my firm and together with Sam we can overcome each of our individual challenges."*

It's the end of a long day and Pavel arrives to take George back to the airport. After they say their goodbyes, Sam is left with Diana where he shares a concern:

*"Diana, this is working out better than I had expected. I truly appreciate your vision and the fact that I can trust you to prioritize my best interests as if they were yours. That means a lot to me. I don't want to seem ungracious, but my board will not like the fact that I'm hitting my numbers with only one client. They will need to see how this is attractive to many firms like yours. Is there anyone else you can introduce me to that would demonstrate an abundance of interest in this environmental modeling solution?"*

Diana acknowledges Sam's challenge and thinks carefully, *"Yes, Sam, let me introduce you to several friends of mine… let's start with Debbie."*

As George settles in on the airplane, he reflects on what has turned out to be an exceptionally productive day. There are four profound learnings that he must communicate to his team as they tackle the EV challenge:

- Changes in velocity are the key to understanding timing.
- Focus on the relevant components of the problem, not all the moving parts.
- Sequencing is the key; what is important when.
- Operate from a position of abundance.

# 38

## PATIENCE

Sam is on his way to visit Simon, the board member and entrepreneur who stood up for him at that crucial board meeting months ago. Since then, Simon has been mentoring Sam with support that has been invaluable.

The plan Sam has hatched with Diana seems to be working, but his anxiety while they wait for results is testing his patience. Sam knows that Simon has a way of calming his nerves and providing the clarity and focus the situation demands.

Sam is excited to meet with Simon at his beach house. His expectation is that of a cavernous sanctuary emblematic of Simon's tremendous success. Upon arrival, however, Sam is surprised by the modest and unassuming house to which his navigation system has guided him. But before he can even validate the destination in his GPS, Simon steps out to greet him with a warm and hearty welcome.

After showing Sam around the humble bungalow, they migrate to an oceanside deck with spectacular views of steep cliffs dropping straight into white sand beaches and the deep blue sea. Sam's jaw opens wide as he takes in the stunning panorama.

Simon then chimes in, *"Wealth consists not in having great possessions, but in having few wants."*

The view of the ocean showcases a natural beauty that is hard to describe. Sam thinks to himself how Simon appears to have transcended material validation with wants of greater substance and value. He silently questions his understanding of wealth and hopes he has the good fortune to make similar judgments in his own life.

Simon then asks Sam how things are going and how he can help. Sam explains how Diana is using the software with twelve of her clients. Additionally, Diana's introduction to Debbie has expanded their reach to five of her firm's clients. Furthermore, Diana has introduced Sam's sales leaders to several other environmental firms in her network. What is most exciting, though, is that the predictive models, based on the rate of change, are working better than he or George ever expected. Everyone seems to be happy... except for Sam.

Feeling safe to share his emotions with his new mentor, Sam relates that he is struggling with anxiety as he waits for implementations to complete and new sales to come through. His stress levels are high and he feels the need to do something instead of just waiting.

Simon tries to calm Sam by letting him know that his strategy is working and everyone seems to be doing their part. He then steps up to the edge of the balcony and motions his arm slowly across the beautiful vista and says to Sam, *"No great thing is created suddenly."*

Sam understands what Simon is trying to tell him, but he is still nervous about the IPO and the challenging timeline that he set forth when pressed by Stephen during that fateful board meeting months ago; *"Simon, you don't get it... what should I be doing? I don't want to be crucified by the board for doing nothing. I know you'll tell me that patience is a virtue, but they aren't paying me to be a passive spectator."*

Simon seats himself in front of Sam and squares his shoulders and eyes with the young executive. After a deep breath and a lengthy pause, he speaks, *"Patience is not a passive activity. Patience requires confidence. Where is it that you lack confidence?"*

Sam is stunned by Simon's words and the deliberate manner of his delivery. He thinks carefully as he ponders where he lacks confidence. After his own long pause, Sam sheepishly admits to Simon that he doesn't know.

Simon methodically walks Sam through everything that is going on right now. The product is working. His sales team is delivering. The environmental model is proving popular and valuable. Everything about his strategy is working. Intent on getting Sam to answer the question he posed, Simon takes a different approach. This time he asks Sam to avoid ruminating on the answer and to just verbally walk through his own analysis.

Sam comes to similar conclusions as Simon. He trusts his team and his product. Everything they are trying to do is within the capabilities of the product and his team. He even trusts his new partner, Diana. Her motives are aligned with his and she is proving to be a capable and virtuous person. His strategy is proving to be sound and resilient. But as he speaks, Sam shares that he fears disappointing the board and is even more scared of letting Sarah down.

Listening carefully to Sam, Simon poses a new question using some of Sam's own words, *"You are now speaking of trust rather than confidence. I agree that trust is necessary for confidence to exist. Who or what don't you trust?"*

*"I guess I'm nervous about the IPO process,"* Sam responds. *"I've never been through one and I don't think that Stephen and I have much in common. I don't know what to expect and I fear that my fate, and that of my family, is in the hands of someone I'm not sure I trust."*

*"Now we're making progress Sam!"* Simon exclaims. *"You've been impatient about all of the things you can influence, but your stress is coming from the one thing you can't control. There is only one way to happiness and that is to make the best use of what is in your power and take the rest as it happens."*

*"That's easy for you to say,"* Sam snaps back quickly.

*"Sam, I don't appreciate your comment. I've got more invested in this company than any other individual and I exert less control over the outcome than you. I do appreciate that my past success would allow me to accommodate a failure more gracefully than you, but you should never assume that failure is something I welcome or even tolerate."*

*"I'm sorry, Simon. I let my emotions get the best of me,"* Sam replies, apologetically.

*"Sam, don't let your fears or your emotions dominate your perspective. Look at the facts. Trust yourself and your judgment. Trust your feelings to alert your intellect, but make sure it is your intellect that guides your responses."*

Sam reverently absorbs Simon's wisdom.

After a long pause, Simon continues his counsel to Sam, *"Patience is the truest form of trust and confidence. Patience will test your convictions and the most powerful source of doubt: yourself. You'll get through this, Sam. I trust you. The board trusts you. Trust yourself."*

# 39

## TRUE NORTH

Deep in the woods of Northern Michigan is where Diana spent her summers as a child. Over the years, she built a special bond with her grandfather when they would go hiking and fishing on warm summer days.

Their favorite spot was a secluded lake set back through the forest behind their cottage. The lake was fed by mountain runoff and heated by thermal springs. The location was quiet and stood at the foot of some of the tallest peaks in the region. The calm waters made for great fishing and even better thinking. It was the ideal quiet place to focus your thoughts.

One of their favorite pastimes was sitting quietly by the edge of the lake. They could sit in silence for hours at a time gazing off into the beauty of this perfect slice of nature. Diana's grandfather would sometimes break the silence with questions for her. Sometimes his questions were deep and sometimes they were silly. Sometimes the questions sounded silly but were quite deep. Her favorite question was:

*"If you could plant a dream into other people's heads... what would that dream be?"*

This question and this day were always a vivid memory for Diana. For some reason, this question was special. Perhaps it was the day –her grandfather's birthday– or perhaps it was the warm sun and the spectacular clear blue sky. Whatever it was, that day was special.

Diana did not need much time to answer her grandfather's question. The answer seemed obvious to her. Her reply was simple and profound,

*"To make sure everyone knows what it is like to have a special place like this to enjoy with someone they love."*

Her grandfather smiled wide and didn't say another word the rest of the time they spent at the lake that day.

As Diana got older, she realized she could ask questions too. Sometimes the questions were silly and sometimes they were really silly. But she always remembered the look on her grandfather's face when he thought quietly before he would answer. The look on his face was peaceful and calm. His gaze would target some unknown object across the lake while he took his time to think. Her grandfather never rushed his response. Eventually his emotionless gaze would narrow before he turned back to Diana with his response.

When her grandfather answered, he would stare deeply into Diana's eyes as if he could see straight through to her soul. His responses were always thoughtful, deliberate, and complete. He was amazing in the way he weaved his reply into some analogy or life experience Diana could relate to. His ability to understand his audience and make a point was masterful.

What was most unique about her grandfather's responses is that they were never really answers, they were a series of questions that led you to an answer of your own. The answers were usually quite simple, but it was the formulation of the questions that would lead you to that answer that must have taken him so long to think through. Diana didn't realize it at the time, but he was teaching her how to think. How to calmly see the world clearly so that she could solve her own problems.

In retrospect, Diana knows the woman she is today was shaped by the conversations she had with her grandfather by their secluded lake. In fact, Diana knows that her love for the environment came from their quiet and thoughtful visits to the place they called "Sofia Point."

She looked forward to those trips out into the woods with her grandfather. He always made her feel special. Sometimes all he did was listen. But she always left the lake feeling one inch taller.

As Diana grew up, visits to the summer cottage became less frequent. And as her grandparents aged, their time in the woods tapered off as well. Eventually, the cottage was vacant and fell into disrepair.

Years later, after her grandfather passed away, the family went up to the cabin to clean out decades of junk and decay. What they found was a lifetime of memories and remembrances.

Diana hadn't been to the cottage since the day she cleaned it out with her family. Somehow, the thought of returning to her happy place without her best buddy was just too sad to contemplate.

Mentally, however, Diana returns to this location on a regular basis. Every time she sees the name of her company displayed above the entrance of her building, she is filled with a sense of pride that reminds her of her heritage and her family history. W.W. Consulting is named after her grandfather William. Moreover, the all-important "True North" story is set at her favorite spot, "Sophia Point."

But today is the day she is returning. She is returning because she realizes she has left something behind. All these years she has selfishly hoarded the beauty of this magical location even though she has shared its significance with so many others.

Months ago, Diana commissioned a construction company to revive the cottage and update it with all the modern conveniences. Diana intends to enjoy the cabin and its beautiful surroundings with friends and family. And with every visit she will also honor the legacy of the special moments she spent with her grandfather.

Today is special because she is celebrating with friends. Last week, Sam was at the stock exchange celebrating his company's successful IPO. And in the last month, George celebrated his first official pre-order for a new electric vehicle transmission and suspension system. Today, she welcomes these friends to her renovated woodland retreat.

The cottage is as grand as Diana remembered as a child. There is plenty of room for Diana, Dean, Sam, Sarah, George, and Grace. All of them are nicely squared away for a long weekend celebration.

After a wonderful dinner, they gather by the campfire to relax and enjoy a clear view of the stars. A fire at dusk is a special experience that is always enjoyable in the northern woods. The process involves stories and drinks while you patiently wait to be enveloped by the rich darkness that illuminates the constellations above.

George takes a moment to thank Diana and Dean for their hospitality. He is grateful for Diana's stewardship through this stressful time. George relates how the pressure of his family's legacy and the responsibility to his community kept him from being clear-eyed about their priorities. He humbly admits that it was only through Diana's calm, clear, and focused approach that he was able to properly prioritize the activities of his team. George always knew timing would be important to their success, but he never realized how important patience and looking at the sequence of events would be to his business. Working with Diana has been one of the best business partnerships of his career. Her advice and counsel make him feel as though he has an unfair advantage.

Sam then shares how nervous he was that he had made a terrible mistake investing so much of his personal savings into his company. He let his confidence and pride keep him from seeing the situation for what it was. He relates how the success of his company and the windfall of their IPO would not have been possible without so many other people. If it wasn't for the support of Sarah, Simon, and his new friends, Diana and George he would not be where he is today. In a voice trembling with emotion, Sam thanks Diana and George for their contributions to his success. Without them he would not have been able to see a clear path forward.

Diana acknowledges the kind words from Sam and George. She is awestruck by the impact she has had on their lives and the communities that depend upon them.

Surrounded by the feelings of gratitude shared by everyone encircling the fire, Diana knows what she must do this evening. Diana tells the story that embodies the ethos of her company and the model by which she lives her life.

## The "True North" Story

A little girl sat with her grandfather at the edge of a lake that was as still as a mirror. They both stared off into the distance and watched the sun slowly lower into the horizon.

The little girl asked a question to her grandfather, *"How do you know when you are right about something and how do you know when to change your mind?"*

He answered back with a question, *"What is North?"*

The little girl pointed back, *"North is where the compass points."*

Her grandfather pulled out a compass. *"Show me where North is."*

*"It's over there,"* she replied, pointing across the lake in the direction of the compass needle.

*"Is that True North?,"* he said, posing yet another question.

*"What's True North?,"* the little girl inquired.

*"The compass points at magnetic North and that is always changing. True North, over there, points to the North Pole which is not the same as magnetic North,"* her grandfather stated calmly pointing his finger toward the North Pole. *"And True North never changes."*

"So what does this have to do with my question?," she asked with a tinge of frustration in her voice.

His reply changed her life forever:

*"Your thoughts on many subjects may change through the years— much like magnetic North changes. Other things will stay firmly planted in your mind like True North. Those thoughts will never change.*

*My understanding of the world around me is like magnetic North— it is always changing. But my love for you is like True North— it will never change.*

*As you grow up, hold your values firm like True North. But your opinions should be more like magnetic North… always able to change. Be careful not to let your emotions or your fears turn opinions into steadfast values. And never let your values sway with the opinions of others."*

As Diana concludes the story, tears are gently rolling down her cheek. She has never shared this story at the same place where she spent summers with her beloved grandfather. But her tears are not those of sadness, they are tears of happiness and profound respect. She is overcome with deep feelings of contentment as she finally reconciles the loss of her grandfather with the realization that his legacy lives on through her.

# PART V

## THE CLEAR PATH FORWARD

My son came home from school one day and said he wanted to play lacrosse. He was in third grade, and we had already had a number of unsuccessful bouts with different sports. I had played club lacrosse in college and was wondering if he had a true interest in the sport or if he was trying to find a way to win my love and attention. I was terrified that I had unknowingly put pressure on him to succeed in sports. That he was desperate for my approval.

I asked him why he was interested in lacrosse and I was extremely nervous about the answer. His explanation transformed me.

He articulately stated that he knew he had not done well trying other sports. If he went back to those sports now, he would be behind the other boys, and they might laugh at him. But lacrosse was a sport that you couldn't start playing until third grade. Because of that, he would be able to start exactly where the other kids started. It was an even playing field. That was his rationale. I was stunned by the flawless clarity of his thinking. He then asked a question that was obviously important to him. He asked if they kept score in lacrosse. He stated clearly that he didn't want to play if they didn't keep score.

At that moment I knew success would always be within his reach. All I had to do was to get out of the way.

I did not see what he saw so clearly. My emotions and fears blinded me from the path forward that was obvious to him. He had a clear understanding of what was important and how he could achieve his goals. His mind was clear.

Once I understood his reasoning, I was excited about playing catch in the backyard and watching him play from the sidelines. That's not quite what happened. When we dropped him off at the first practice, one of the coaches asked if anyone knew how to play the game. The rest is history. I coached for nearly ten years and served as the administrator of several affiliated organizations.

Although I was busy running a company, coaching made me better in every way. I became a better leader, a better teacher, a better father, and a better person.

The part of coaching I enjoyed most was the moment in almost every player's progression when everything finally "clicked." There was a visible moment when the game slowed down for them. Instead of running around in a panic, they would execute basic skills, observe their surroundings, consider options, and calmly make decisions. Fear stopped governing the way they saw the game, and things that used to be perceived as obstacles could now become opportunities.

Once players hit this inflection point, their ability to be "coachable" grew exponentially. They were ready for new information, more options, and higher levels of performance. Every coach knows how rewarding it is when athletes get to the point where things seem effortless.

I'm ashamed to admit that I was relieved when my daughter chose to play soccer instead of lacrosse. Even though she probably felt deprived that I was never her coach, she rewarded me with the ability to just be a dad and a cheerleader for her. It is a gift she certainly didn't sign up to give, but it was a gift of immense value to me.

Just as my son's rationale taught me about having a clear vision by separating the core issue from my emotional reactions, my daughter allowed me to observe something different and equally important.

My daughter was a talented athlete, but even her competitive travel teams were not always in a position to win. I sometimes wondered how she stayed motivated when the reward of winning was not there to accompany all the hard work. Of course, she wanted to win, but something else was motivating her dedication to the sport. She enjoyed the challenge and the process of improving herself. I did not initially see what she saw so clearly. You are always winning if you are improving.

Through their involvement in sports, both of my children provided me with many important perspectives that greatly influenced how I thought about what I was doing at work.

During this same time, my business career was in full swing. The success I was having and the team I was working with was championship grade. They were truly glorious years.

I began to make connections between my coaching and my business. I noticed when the "game slowed down" for consultants on our team. They began to listen better. Their creativity soared. They were more confident. They were more engaged.

I also noticed how attitudes improved when consultants became passionate about developing their skills. When employees moved beyond outcomes and were motivated to perfect their craft, they too became more confident and engaged. The balance between skills, emotions, and behaviors all contribute to a higher level of understanding and performance. But a desire to learn and the curiosity to pursue feedback is what drives true excellence.

I even noticed these same patterns with clients and people I was mentoring. In each case, as they grew more confident with themselves and the issues facing them, their thinking was clearer and success was soon to follow.

The final section of this book is dedicated to the "flow" state that can be achieved in business when people have a clear path forward (Csikszentmihalyi, 2008). This is when the efforts you put forth have disproportionate impacts. This is when you create your own clarity and begin to accomplish more with less effort.

# 40

## CONSCIOUS COMPETENCE

*"If this is going to work, you have to let someone else manage your team."* That is what I was told when we discussed a new strategy with my business partners. We had decided to spin-off a software startup from our consulting firm to capitalize on an exciting market opportunity we were pursuing. The prospect of creating a new business with a much higher valuation was a great strategy and an even better investment of our time and treasure.

My role in this strategy was to replace the sales revenue we expected to lose when two of my partners, the founders of our consulting firm, shifted their focus to the new startup. For the strategy to work, I had to give up managing my Chicago team to focus entirely on sales. It was one of the most heart-wrenching decisions of my career. I never liked sales, but I was good at it. I much preferred leading our large team of consultants. The relationships I enjoyed with my team were rich and strong. They were family.

However, we knew that other capable leaders could manage the team, but nobody else had the skills to replace what we lost when our co-founder Andrew shifted his focus away from sales. The decision was the right decision, but it felt awful. Give up what you love to do something you hate.

Other than working harder, I had no idea how I would double my results to keep our plan on track. I had to do my part, but I was terrified that I would fail. And in this case, failure would be devastating for the work family I felt I was abandoning. I couldn't let them down– failure was not an option. I dedicated myself to mastering my new craft and delivering the results we needed to keep the strategy in play.

In the year that passed, I established a new family of client relationships that served our company and our business well. I had fulfilled my obligation and I was beyond relieved. I was headed into a meeting with Andrew expecting a pat on the back and congratulations for a job well done. I did not receive the triumphant response I had anticipated.

For as tough and demanding as he was, Andrew was a fair and benevolent leader who brought out the best in people who valued peak performance. I loved the challenge of trying to live up to his exceedingly high standards, a fact he knew all too well.

Andrew congratulated me on a job well done, but he did not allow me to bask in my accomplishment. He quickly responded with a question that changed the course of my professional career, *"But can you teach other people to do what you just did?"*

After a moment of disbelief from his seemingly ungrateful inquiry, I pondered his question. It was a fantastic question. My answer was simple: *"No."*

Andrew then asked how long it would take for me to be able to teach someone else what I was doing. I stated that it would probably take another year for me to pay attention to what I was doing so that I could be aware of what led to my success. He responded in his typical fashion, *"You're not done."*

Truth be told, I was a bit upset with Andrew. But he was right, and his question was fascinating. I was curious to know the answer.

And curiosity would be the driving force and the key that unlocked the secrets fueling my success.

Instinctually I knew what to say and how to say it, but I had no idea why it worked. I spent the next eighteen months paying close attention to the events that would trigger an instinctual response as well as which specific approaches were most effective. In order to develop a stronger understanding of my gut instincts, I took a deep interest in psychology, persuasion, and behavioral economics.

There were two incredible outcomes from this very deliberate process. The first outcome is that I discovered a way to work less and accomplish more to a degree that was unimaginable. In less than one day per week I was now accomplishing goals that previously required a whole week. This benefit allowed me to allocate additional time to read more books and deepen my understanding of networking, powerful relationships, and human behavior.

The second outcome was the more profound revelation. The temptation to stop the process of discovery once you start getting results is incredible. Only the truly curious and committed person persists in their quest for the reward that lies just beyond competence, Conscious Competence.

Conscious Competence is a heightened awareness of small details that have disproportionate impacts and minute adjustments that effortlessly nudge people toward productive outcomes. It is a benefit that is realized by recognizing the proper sequencing of events and timing of one's actions. It is the calm that supports the patience necessary to listen carefully to the world around you. It is a powerful understanding that seems unfair once you experience it.

Aside from these two rather remarkable benefits, you may ask yourself, why are we introducing a new concept this late in our journey toward clarity. It is because Conscious Competence is the penultimate waypoint on our path toward clarity.

# 41

## BUSINESS WISDOM®

Wisdom is the ultimate intellectual ambition that is beyond the limits of any individual to comprehend. To understand wisdom is to accept that it is something that can never be fully realized. It is not an accomplishment or an achievement for which a title is conferred. Wisdom is not about knowing things, it is about wanting to know about things. Wisdom is the discipline of thinking clearly.

Throughout this book, wisdom is showcased in the stories of Diana, Sam, and George. Diana's grandfather William is presented as the perfect example of wisdom in this book. His thoughtful and patient questioning intentionally mirrors a Socratic dialogue. William's masterful application of the Socratic method is an ideal example of Conscious Competence in action. The important lesson with his character is how he uses his wisdom to teach Diana how to think clearly for herself.

Another wise figure embedded in the stories of this book is Simon. His character is modeled after the Stoic philosopher Epictetus. One of the main lessons we learn through Simon is how to challenge dogmatic thinking and focus our energy on that which we can control. His mentorship helps Sam separate his emotions from the facts so that he can see a clear path forward.

Other characters such as George, Dean, Diana's mother-in-law, and Pavel have opportunities to demonstrate their own Conscious Competence and wisdom throughout the book. Every character adds something to the tapestry of experiences that shape our view of the challenges they face.

But the key person demonstrating wisdom is Diana. Her journey is important because she develops her wisdom, and thus her clarity, throughout the book. We get to join her as she solves her own problems and begins to help others with their issues. We see her grow from a place of doubt and weakness into the strong and confident visionary that leads others out of their own darkness. Diana illuminates the clear path forward for her business, her clients, and her new friends, Sam and George.

Wisdom is all around us, yet we frequently do not see it. It often takes a mentor or a muse to guide us toward that which we do not yet see. This book is intended to be that guide for you. Within these pages is a blueprint for diagnosing and addressing the most common business problems– Business Wisdom.

If you consider the journey we've taken together through this book, you will realize that there is a deliberate process we have followed. In Part I, we spend time understanding the most common business symptoms and how they present themselves as warning signs for underlying problems. This is important because dealing with symptoms can distract us from addressing core issues that only get worse with neglect. Each of these symptoms is examined from multiple perspectives to showcase the variety of ways in which they manifest themselves. Furthermore, we use medical analogies to help cement our understanding into a mental model that is more familiar. And to provide an even richer context, we track the same process through the personal relationship we build with Diana and her story.

As we progress into Part II, we introduce the core business problems that are often overshadowed by the symptoms in Part I. We explore how we make decisions and how we often jump to conclusions before we fully understand our circumstances. Sam's journey through this process is exceptionally important. His story mirrors so much of what I've observed through my years as a consultant and advisor to companies of all shapes and sizes.

Of additional value is how we identify several important developmental skills often prescribed as analgesics for the business pains we experience. It should be noted, however, we never devalue the importance of symptoms or skills as we explore each core issue in depth. What we aim to do is showcase the importance of methodically identifying underlying core issues amidst the many business distractions we face daily.

Additionally, we don't attempt to make this book the authoritative guide on how to solve all business problems. As stated earlier, there are countless books that address each of these core problems, but there are few, if any, that help us identify which problem is at the heart of the matter. This is the purpose of this book and the reason why you may wish to develop Business Wisdom.

As we progress into Part III, we enter what could be considered the 300-level college course on Business Wisdom. This section introduces the most nuanced aspects of diagnosing business problems and where we truly advance our understanding of clear thinking. These chapters focus on the most impactful elements that skew or sharpen how we view our circumstances. We outline the tremendous influence context and assumptions have upon our reasoning. We also introduce how common misconceptions with numbers distort information we may consider to be factual. Finally, we tackle the elephant in the room –our emotions– and how they can lead us astray.

But Part III contains one of the most powerful takeaways from this entire book– the power of curiosity. Curiosity is the key that turns context, assumptions, numbers, and emotions into powerful allies in our search for clarity. Curiosity opens doors to new ideas and new perspectives that can sharpen our critical thinking. Curiosity is the vital first waypoint on the path toward clarity.

Curiosity is what makes George's story so important. George is insanely curious. George finds inspiration in the most uncommon places. And while Diana finds similar inspirations through unlikely events, George is different. Diana's success is predicated on the fact that her mind is open to new ideas that cross her path. George's success is due to a deliberate pursuit of fresh perspectives and deeper understanding. George may not be consciously aware of the role curiosity plays in his success, but it is obvious that he is methodical in the way he unleashes his curious mind.

Part IV is all about time. Time is the single most rigid constraint on all our desires, yet it is the one element that holds the answer to a calmer and clearer picture of the path forward. Re-establishing our relationship with time is a pivotal waypoint in our journey toward clarity.

Sequencing, timing, and patience are the keys to changing our relationship with time. This is where the stories of Diana, Sam, and George become very important. Abstract concepts such as these typically lose meaning when they are spoken about in an academic sense. But when you put these concepts into the rich stories of the characters we identify with, their impact is more meaningful.

When we understand and embrace the importance of sequencing, we learn how to break down our problems and focus our energy on the issues that require our attention first. Dean's emergency room story is the analogy that drives this point into your mind. By focusing our attention, we avoid the panic that urgency often incites. And when we heighten our awareness, hear the unheard and see the unseen, we find the perfect timing that yields a superior result with far less effort. Timing is not elusive to the observant person who listens carefully.

The final element that changes our relationship with time is patience. Patience demands self-discipline over our most corrosive emotions. In order to be patient, we must overcome the fear of being victimized, the guilt of indecision, and self-doubt in our own capabilities. Patience requires confidence and confidence comes from trust in both people and process, but most of all, patience requires trust in ourselves. When we take the steps to permit our own patience, the game slows down, our emotions subside, and obstacles become opportunities.

There is a saying within the military special operations community that encapsulates the benefit gained from proper sequencing, timing, and patience: *"Slow is smooth, smooth is fast."*

In Part V we do more than review what we've learned in the first four sections, we introduce the final two waypoints on our journey toward clarity. It is only through the concepts and stories of the prior sections that we are ready to accept concepts such as Conscious Competence and Business Wisdom. Both concepts build upon everything else that we have learned and provide the important context that illuminates the clear path forward. Conscious Competence is the key ingredient needed to develop our Business Wisdom; and Business Wisdom is the process through which we obtain clarity.

In time, anyone can develop their own Business Wisdom and an endless supply of clarity. All that is needed is the time and space to develop confidence in yourself.

# 42

## ONE INCH TALLER

There is a fateful moment of betrayal that is engrained in many of our lives. That moment takes place on the day we learned to ride a bike with two wheels. The process starts with an acknowledgment that "it's time" to make the jump to two wheeled locomotion. A pensive interest and a measured level of excitement is accompanied by haunting fears of twisted wreckage and broken bones.

With cajoling and encouragement from our most trusted confidants, our emotions fluctuate between excitement and panic as the mechanical process of removing training wheels builds into a mountain of dramatic tension.

The betrayal begins when the instructor –usually a parent or sibling– promises to not let go of the bike while running alongside. *"Don't worry! I won't let go… I promise…"* is a phrase that is almost universal. Just as universal is the fact that the person you trusted most does, in fact, let go.

What happens next is as predictable as the sun rising in the East. After a brief moment of independent gliding, powered by the steady hand of your trusted instructor, the realization sets in that you are on your own. Panic sets in. Pedaling stops. And so does stability.

The loss of speed and control inevitability ends in a crash that can range from gentle to brutal. Even if the pedaling continues and victory is in sight, the skill for stopping gracefully is inconveniently reserved for lesson number two.

What is fascinating is that an exceptionally interesting phenomenon usually takes place during this process. Even though a profound betrayal of trust has taken place, it is overshadowed by the personal growth that has come forth in the form of a new-found capability that has been realized.

Moments of personal growth result in feelings of accomplishment, confidence, and belief. But how does a betrayal of trust turn fears and doubts into confidence and belief?

As with the bicycle example, our moments of growth are frequently supported by a person that helps us overcome our fears, build our confidence, and provide us the extra boost we need to take on the risks that accompany any sort of growth. These people may be parents, siblings, supervisors, mentors, or coaches. Regardless of their formal relationship with us, the common theme is that we trust them.

But moments of personal growth aren't always tied to success. In many cases, our failures are the driving forces in how we learn. So how do these influential people in our lives retain our trust when they push us into danger, deceive us with feelings of security, and set us up for failure?

They can do this because they get us to trust ourselves.

The ability of someone to help us understand how we can trust ourselves rather than someone or something else is a powerful lesson in life. The analogy to training wheels could not be more complete.

When we are learning to ride a bike, we do not trust our own ability to balance. Balance is a sensation that is far too complicated to understand with words or instruction. It is the training wheels that we trust to keep us from falling over.

However, by experiencing the sensation of balance and realizing that balance is a state you can create, we are able to teach people to ride a bicycle. Our trusted influencers know that balance must be experienced to be understood. The person learning to ride a bicycle does not. It is the mentor or the coach that helps us experience something new in order to open our eyes to expanded possibilities.

As Benjamin Franklin once said:

---

*"Tell me and I'll forget.*
*Teach me and I'll remember.*
*Involve me and I learn."*

---

In business, the goal for any coach or mentor is to help people reach for something they lack the confidence to do on their own. Initially, they may lean on their coach for detailed instruction and advice. In times of failure, the instructor is there to ensure lessons are learned and confidence is restored. Eventually, the wisdom of the coach speaks to the individual even when they are not present.

It sounds easy, but it is not. Good coaching and mentoring require patience, empathy, and love. But if there is one rule of thumb, it should be this: Mentors, advisors, and coaches should aspire to end every conversation with the recipient feeling like they are one inch taller.

**One inch taller.** This is the credo I aspire to when coaching and advising clients. Every interaction and every discussion should provide the receiving party with greater clarity in their purpose, confidence in themselves, and conviction in their motivation.

There are few things as satisfying as seeing someone you care for find their own internal strength. The satisfaction intensifies when you see how personal growth manifests itself in ways that are physically observable. A voice is more assertive. A stride is more powerful. Posture and body language suggest an internal confidence.

The satisfaction evolves into pride when you witness someone recover from a setback on their own. The ability to rebound from failure is a sign of resilience, maturity, and confidence.

And while I would like to think that ego never plays a role for mentors and coaches, it is always nice for your efforts to be recognized and appreciated. Perhaps the ultimate compliment is when you are told that your voice was in their head guiding their next move.

When you spend time helping others see clearly, it also helps you see clearly. As the proverb goes, *"steel sharpens steel, and one friend sharpens another"* (Proverbs 27:17). The gift for any parent, mentor, coach, or leader is to receive the wisdom that is gained through interactions with those you care for deeply.

In a broader context, it is important to recognize that wisdom only comes into existence once it has been shared with another person. Therefore, it is the responsibility of anyone who wishes to pursue wisdom to share freely what they know and to be open to what they may learn. And that is why a good life is not lived in solitude, but in the service of others. Hence, a good life begins by trusting in yourself to help others feel one inch taller.

---

## Want to help someone else feel One Inch Taller?

Get this book for a friend, associate, or family member!

If you have found this book valuable and know others who would find it useful, consider buying them a copy as a gift. Special bulk discounts are available if you would like your whole team or organization to benefit from reading this. Just contact claritybook@rafti.com or visit www.businesswisdom.com/clarity

# 43

## MERAKI

There is a Greek word that does not singularly exist in the English language. It is a shame because it is a wonderful word. That word is *Meraki*.

The rough translations to the word is "gusto" or "passion" do not quite do it justice. It is more properly defined as:

**meraki** [may-rah-kee] (noun)

The soul, the creativity, and the love one puts into what one does. It is when the essence of who you are is put into what you do.

Meraki is not necessary for clarity or Business Wisdom. However, meraki can be the fuel that provides the energy to persist, support, and lead others along the clear path forward.

The key to meraki is that it requires none of the scarce resources that constrain what we can achieve in business. Financial resources and budgets are limited. Talent is always in short supply. Time is precious.

With meraki, however, we tap into soul, creativity, and love. These are three resources with an endless supply. To empower our soul all we need to do is let people be themselves. To unleash creativity, all we need to do is let them think freely. And to bring love into the equation, all we need to do is be unafraid to tap into the most powerful and positive force we possess as human beings.

The clear path forward is the path of less work and greater accomplishment. The clear path forward is the path of progress. The clear path forward is not always easy to see -but it is there- paved with the soul, creativity, and love we all possess in abundance.

# REVIEW INQUIRY

Hey, it's Jim here.

I hope you've enjoyed the book, finding it both useful and fun. I have a favor to ask you.

Would you consider giving it a rating wherever you bought the book? Online book stores are more likely to promote a book when they feel good about its content and reader reviews are a great barometer for a book's quality.

So please go to the website of wherever you bought the book, search for my name and the book title, and leave a review. If able, perhaps consider adding a picture of you holding the book. That increases the likelihood your review will be accepted!

Many thanks in advance,

Jim Vaselopulos

# WOULD YOU LIKE TO GET SOME CLARITY DIRECTLY FROM JIM VASELOPULOS?

Book Jim Now!

Jim Vaselopulos accepts a limited number of speaking, coaching and sales training engagements each year. To learn how you can bring his message to your organization, email claritybook@rafti.com or visit www.raftiadvisors.com.

# ACKNOWLEDGMENTS

I hope you enjoyed reading this book as much as I enjoyed writing it. And while writing can be seen as a tedious and laborious effort, it became a joyful effort for me. Part of the joy I experienced was that my parents and grandparents were never with me more than while I was writing. They have all since passed, but their voices, values and wisdom helped shape what you are reading today.

It is hard to fully understand the concept of unconditional love without experiencing the type of love that goes with a large extended family. I am grateful for the love and support of my big Greek family.

I am also grateful for my grandfather and my uncles who served in our military. My maternal grandfather Sam, who fought in two Balkan Wars, came to America and promptly served his new adopted country back in Europe in WWI. My paternal grandfather helped an entire region in rural Greece survive the perils of German occupation and the terrible civil war that ensued after WWII. All these men embodied the Greek ethos of freedom that dates back to Thermopylae, through to Greek Independence and the valiant efforts of the Greek resistance in WWII. The concept that the freedoms I enjoy are paid for by the sacrifices of others will never be lost on me.

I am grateful for the support of my dear friend Jan Rutherford. His guidance, support, and mentorship have been invaluable in my journey and in the writing of this book. Whether it was his

life-changing crucible expeditions or his invitation to join him as
co-host of The Leadership Podcast, he helped me make the transition from doer to teacher. His mentorship and friendship allowed
me to realize a new path forward where I could coach others toward
their own clarity.

Writing a book is a long and unforgiving process. I am thankful
for the early inspiration I received from folks like Andy LaCivita
and Sarah Victory. I am thankful to Todd Sattersten who played a
significant role in helping me write this particular book. Todd is a
fantastic thinking partner who helped me find my voice and write
the right book. And many thanks to Allie Pleiter who helped me
develop the discipline necessary to write a book rather than think
about writing a book. I was blessed with an awesome neighbor Joe
Corrado who helped me mercilessly edit copy into a more readable
form. And I am grateful for the support and friendship of my
assistant Kim Billings. She keeps my calendar and helps provide
the discipline necessary to manage my busy schedule and find time
to write.

There are many people in your life that play the important
role of "momentary benefactor" such as Dr. Susan Nelson, Neal
Keating, or Ken Fox. Other people provide changes in direction
that shape your life in significant ways. Without my college roommate Mike McDaniel, I never would have been introduced to the
sport of lacrosse and one of my most influential coaches Dick
Evans. Without my childhood friend Mark Ashbrook, I never
would have been exposed to computers and many other things
a first-generation American never gets to experience. Mark also
brought me into our fraternity where I made great friendships that
last to this day. If I hadn't gone to the Allen-Bradley informational
seminar with my fraternity brother Dave "Farley" McMorran, my
life would be vastly different. And without the help of many others
like John Davis, Tom Varga, Jeff Pitts, Tony Zilla, Brian Fitzpatrick,

Doug Meier, Todd Krone, Bob Reed, and others, I may not have graduated. And thanks to my post-collegiate roommates Rodger Runyan and Jay Tamblingson, I met my wonderful wife Dana at the Kentucky Derby. And without Dave Kintzer, Steve Bohn, Tyler Malewicki, Mark Loewes, Steve Hadaway, Mike Gralinski, Bob Tangredi, Tom Meyer, Shawn McCall, Phil Trabucco, and Phil Faris, coaching would never have been the learning experience it became for me.

I have had many business partners through the years that have provided me with a wealth of experiences to draw from as I counsel others on their entrepreneurial journeys. None were as impactful as Andrew Lauter and Bruce Bellak. They were exceptionally demanding, but their legendary high standards were necessary to bring out my very best. I am grateful for our time together.

It is no surprise that the heroine woven into the stories is a strong woman. I have been fortunate to have many amazing women in my life. My mother, my grandmothers, and many aunts have been wonderful influences on me. My sisters, Mary Ellen and Patricia, have always modeled great behavior and have always been there with love and unwavering support. Finally, I would not have become the man I am today without the unconditional love and support of my mother. I am grateful for the amazing women in my life.

I am eternally grateful for my wonderful and supportive parents. I owe my success to the foundation they provided and the values they instilled into our entire family. Their influence is ever present in the pages of this book. Having lost them both in recent years, they were never far away as I wrote. They guided my thoughts and showed up in the actions and statements of many characters represented in the stories. The gift of clarity that I have tried to share in the pages of this book was originally given to me through their wisdom and unconditional love.

My greatest accomplishments in life and my most important teachers have been my children. My wife Dana and I have been blessed with two wonderful children (Spyros and Emily) with bright minds and loving hearts. Their curiosity keeps us on our toes and their humor keeps us young. They are our pride and joy.

And, of course, the most important person in my life is my wife, Dana. She is indeed my better half. She never ceases to amaze me with her human insights and her common-sense instincts. Her razor-sharp wit keeps me laughing and her down-to-earth values keep me grounded. But what is most amazing about her is the depth of her caring and love for others. I am a better person because of her.

I am eternally grateful for the spiritual guidance of my mother Katherine, my grandmother (γιαγιά) Evanthia and the wonderful people I've met in the Greek Orthodox Church. They all played a part in my deep appreciation of what it means to be a Christian in the Greek Orthodox faith. That foundation allows me to persevere in the face of great challenges, to stand firm in times of uncertainty, to seek the light in others, and to live a life of Stoic discipline along the straight and narrow path.

In the enduring words of my grandmother Evanthia:

*"Work hard, tell the truth, do the right thing."*

# EASTER EGGS

Anyone who knows me is aware of how much I enjoy movie quotes. I can barely remember most of the classes I took in college, but I have a foolish level of recall for movie quotes.

In my professional career, I would entertain myself during meetings by throwing out timely movie quotes to lighten the mood or make a point stick. Over time, I learned to weave them naturally into the conversation and scan the participants for subtle acknowledgments of the artful insertion. A gentle head nod would often make my day.

Occasionally, I would challenge myself to get through a whole meeting only speaking with quotes from movies. Since the focus of the meeting always took precedence, it was a guarantee that success was a lofty goal. However, the challenge was always fun and occasionally led to the rare "perfect game."

In the course of writing this book, I've inserted several Easter Eggs that go way beyond movie quotes. In some instances, these Easter Eggs were for my entertainment and in other cases they were ways to show subtle appreciation for important people, places and events in my life.

Regardless of their purpose, each one of these Easter Eggs represents a level of intentionality that can be both symbolic and purposeful.

An example is embedded in our first story. All of the characters have names that start with the letter D. It just so happens that all of my wife Dana's siblings have names that start with the letter D. This is a small tribute to her and her family. They are wonderful people with grounded values and a great sense of humor.

Another example is the reference to the often-repeated quote from the low-brow comedy *Anchorman*– "sixty percent of the time it works every time."

If you are interested in more stories, more business wisdom and a full list of Easter Eggs, sign up for the Business Wisdom newsletter at www.businesswisdom.com

# ABOUT THE AUTHOR

 Jim Vaselopulos is a C-level business advisor and executive coach with a proven record as a leader, strategist, rainmaker, and expert in new business development. With his principled leadership, visionary approach, and effective execution, Jim has successfully established new companies and transformed underperforming organizations. As the founder of Rafti Advisors, Jim assists early-stage businesses in launching successfully, growth-stage enterprises in accelerating their progress, and established organizations in navigating complex challenges and strategic shifts.

He teaches sales and professional development and frequently speaks on the subjects of leadership and innovation. Jim is also the co-host of The Leadership Podcast and volunteers regularly with business incubators and veterans groups. He graduated from the University of Illinois with a B.S. in Mechanical Engineering and earned his MBA at Marquette University. Jim is a dedicated husband and father of two wonderful children with his wife, Dana.

Jim can be reached at:
Website: www.raftiadvisors.com
Email: claritybook@rafti.com

Made in the USA
Columbia, SC
12 January 2025

50736738R00174